Where
Two or Three
Are Gathered
Someone Spills
The
Milk

Where Two or Three Are Gathered Someone Spills The Milk

Tom Mullen

FRIENDS UNITED PRESS

Richmond, Indiana

Library of Congress Cataloging-in-Publication Data

Mullen, Thomas James, 1934-
  Where two or three are gathered, someone spills the milk.

  Reprint. Originally published: Where 2 or 3 are gathered together,
someone spills his milk. Waco, Tex.: Word Books, 1973.
  1. Meditations.   I. Title.
BV4832.2.M86   1986   242   86-14322
ISBN 0-913408-95-6

Quotation from the Revised Standard Version of the Bible, copyrighted 1946, 1952,
© 1971, 1973 by the Division of Christian Education of the National Council of
Churches of Christ in the United States of America, is used by permission.

THE LION SLEEPS TONIGHT (Wimoweh) (Mbube), new lyric and revised music
by Hugo Peretti, Luigi Creatore, George Weiss and Albert Stanton, based on a
song by Solomon Linda and Paul Campbell, TRO- © copyright 1952 and 1961
Folkways Music Publishers, Inc., New York, N.Y. and used by permission.

To my brother, Frank

CONTENTS

CONTENTS

PREFACE

It is important to make clear what this book is not, as buying it with wrong expectations is second only to not buying it at all. It is not a book of advice, such as "How to find God while carrying out the garbage." Nor is it a book of positive thoughts which will make us better people for having read them.

It is a collection of brief meditations about a whole bunch of little and large frustrations, most of which the author has experienced himself, although a few are based on the observations of others. The only person, for sure, who has been helped by the book is the writer himself, as transforming his own molehills into mountains has helped him keep his sanity a while longer. If anyone else is helped by this book, it will probably be because humor shows people they are not alone. I spill milk. You spill milk. All God's children spill milk, and when we learn how universal this experience is, we'll be able to move beyond crying over it.

This does not mean we'll be able to keep from spilling it. It does mean that we may be able to laugh about it, at least if it doesn't land in our laps. Finding some humor in our problems is the next best thing to solving them. This attitude, furthermore, represents a stance toward life which is essentially a Christian one, as it is essential to the ongoing, daily process of affirming God's creation, warts and all.

Considerable gratitude is hereby extended to my wife, Nancy, and our four children, Sarah, Martha, Bret, and Ruth. They and their several partners in mischief, which include a dog, five aquaria of fish, one frog, and a guinea pig, have provided considerable material for this book. Besides, they think what I write is great, an attitude which shows a complete lack of objectivity, for which the author thanks God.

Appreciation is extended also to *Quaker Life* for permission to include some of the material from a monthly column, "Mullin' It Over," a feature of the magazine which was a threat to its dignity for some time. I am also grateful to Wil Stanton for his clever article in *Ladies Home Journal*, "How to Tell the Democrats from the Republicans," November, 1962. Discovering it in a stack of old magazines inspired one of the meditations and provided the substance of the one entitled "On Election Year Tensions."

Thanks, also, to R. C. Urquhart, who presented much of the material in "On Giving Devotions" as part of a talk at a national Presbyterian meeting. Any suits for plagiarism should first be directed toward Samuel Emerick, Director of Yokefellow Institute, who taped the devotional and played it at meetings all over America. I stole it from him.

Dorothea Toney, supersecretary at the Earlham School of Religion, typed the manuscript and spared the reader considerable pain in advance by her editorial comments. She deserves a better fate than trying to read my handwriting, as well as a genuine expression of thanks.

Finally, I am grateful to my brother, Frank, who has been kind enough to offer absolutely no advice on the writing of this book. He continues to hold a slight lead over my mother as the living American who has purchased the most copies of my previous books, but he has been helpful in another way of which he may not even be aware. He has lived his life, in good times and bad, with faith and good humor, demonstrating that the two go together and providing ample reason for dedicating this book to him, with love.

Tom Mullen

ON
THE BIRTH
OF A
SECOND CHILD

When the first child is born into a family, great rejoicing occurs. Baby showers are given for the mother who, during pregnancy, is treated by her husband with great tenderness. In-laws are transformed into grandparents by the birth, and as a result they spend large sums of money to buy presents for the tiny creature who has done so much to upgrade their status.

Pictures by the score are taken of the first baby. The little one is photographed on bear rugs and rugs bare, and each snapshot is greeted by relatives with exclamations ranging from "ooh" to "ahh," as if the sight of a baby has caused temporary brain damage. Meticulous attention is given to hygienic matters, too, as baby's health is a major concern. Bottles are carefully sterilized, of course, and every morsel of food that is directed toward his little mouth is treated with the same scientific precision that Louis Pasteur exercised in wiping out epidemics.

Should baby drop his pacifier, it will be immediately snatched from his chubby hands and thoroughly sterilized or even replaced with a new one before it will be allowed to return to those sacred and gumless walls. Some new parents, in fact, are so germ-conscious they wear hygienic masks while feeding or changing their child, a procedure which prevents contamination but may also cause baby to think he is being raised by the Lone Ranger and Tonto.

Such behavior is completely understandable. After all, there really is nothing quite like a first baby. At least that is what rookie parents think—until they have another child, at which time they discover that second babies are a lot like first ones. Or, to put it another way, while the baby is new, the routine by this time is old, and considerable glamor has departed from the experience.

The second child in a family is treated much the same way the second voyage to the moon has been treated: it is a major achievement, but it's been done before. The only way a second child can get special recognition is to be of a different sex from the first baby, and even then he or she usually misses out on the showers, the exciting announcements, and all those relatives gathered around taking pictures. What he can look forward to is a lifetime of hand-me-down clothes.

Changing diapers, an experience that quickly loses its charm even with the first child, becomes a matter of drudgery with a second baby. Whereas child number one was hovered over by concerned parents ready to provide a fresh diaper for his powdered bottom at the earliest grunt, the second kid may have to knock over a lamp to catch his parents' attention. If he drops his pacifier, which is probably a used one anyhow, his dad will plug it immediately back into the child's mouth or, at best, knock off the big germs with his finger like a smoker flicking ashes from a cigar.

Indeed, if the parents are students of child psychology, they will concentrate their energies toward the preparation of the first child for the arrival of the second. Lengthy explanations about the shape of mummy's tummy will be offered, and when the new brother or sister is brought home from the hospital, the parents will pay primary attention to their first-born so that, as the psychology books warn, "the older siblings will not resent the seeming intrusion of the new baby."

Thus, it ought not surprise us that studies of second children reveal that they are usually more competitive than first children. They have to be to survive. They work harder, play harder, and strive for recognition with more intensity. They learn to live with the realities of being somebody's younger brother or sister, of riding used bicycles, and of acting happy when mom presents them with sister's old coat. Second children can understand Jacob's attitude toward Esau, as they sometimes feel they will either have to become president of a bank or rob one to be recognized in their own right.

It is important to note, however, that many second children do survive, with joy, in spite of the accident of their births. Child number two has the benefit of the experience his parents acquired while experimenting on his older brother or sister. He will be stuck by fewer diaper pins, partly because he won't be changed as often and partly because he will be toilet-trained earlier, as the thrill of showing his cute bare bottom to the neighbors will have long since passed. He will create less panic when he cries, and generally he will be the beneficiary of fewer parental blunders than his older brother or sister. The second child, in fact, will teach his mother and father something that they were uncertain about until he appeared on the scene, namely, that another child can be loved as much as the first one and honored for his own individuality—just like real people.

Remember that it was the second child, the prodigal son, for whom the fatted calf was killed and a feast prepared. Surely this indicates that they are deeply loved, and they ought not to have to run away in order to discover this fact. On this they can bet their britches—even if they are secondhand.

GOD OF JACOB *and* ESAU, Help us love our children as individuals. We thank You for all second children who, because they are number two, try harder but don't need to in Your eyes. In the name of Him who showed us the prodigal son was deeply loved. Amen.

ON
MEALTIME
TOGETHERNESS

One of the great insights into the Christian faith is the sacramental view of life. This means, in other words, that many occasions are holy, and that *all* meals can be experiences of communion—not *just* those symbolic ones done in church with the use of tiny glasses and bits of unleavened bread.

One wonders, however, in moments of unfaith, if the Christians who have promoted this particular idea have been married and had four children ranging in age between four and thirteen. An honest appraisal of many such families at mealtime would undoubtedly test the theological accuracy of the idea and raise the question, "*That* is a sacramental occasion???"

It must be admitted that a "mood of worship" is sometimes destroyed as the siblings argue over whose turn it is to bless the food. It is further damaged when the four-year-old enters what might be called her "prayer filibuster"—a seemingly unending process of blessing, by name, every item on the table, each child in her nursery school, things in general, principalities, powers, and her pet turtle.

Children sometimes spill things, too. More accurately stated, children sometimes manage not to spill things, although seldom. Indeed, some families have seriously considered spilling things deliberately, reasoning that once *that* is taken care of they can get on with the meal. Where two or three are gathered together, someone will spill his milk.

Many parents wonder, also, why at least one child in every family inevitably needs to go to the bathroom at mealtime—not before or after, but during. It can easily be explained when families are eating in restaurants, as fascination with public rest rooms is one of the earliest learned traits of childhood. But why at home? Modern science has no answer, and religion can only assume that it is a demonic attempt to destroy family unity.

The sacramental quality of mealtime is not encouraged, either, when one or more children do not remain in their chairs, but wander from place to place to compare food or slip their unwanted vegetables to the dog, who doesn't want them either, a circumstance which can make for a rather messy floor. Given the major problem of getting an entire family to the table at the same time in the first place, children who eat in the stance of Olympic runners preparing to run the hundred-meter dash do not fit the picture that *Better Homes and Gardens* intended as the model of gracious living.

And yet—as far from the ideal as it is, there may be more truth in the idea that mealtime is a sacramental occasion than there seems. A family that can live with each other's idiosyncrasies can discover joy, one of the main ingredients in communion with God and each other. Who is to say that a prayer for the renewed health of three sick guppies by an eight-year-old is not just as efficacious as one in King James English quoted verbatim from the *Book of Common Prayer?* In fact, which is more common?

Love for each other, closeness with each other, the touching and the teasing, the sharing and the spilling—all may be present along with the Living Christ. True, He may *not* be present either, any more than He may *not* be present at high mass in St. John's Cathedral. We, in fact, cannot control His Presence.

Mealtime for many of us can be more sacramental than it is, possibly by practicing better habits of discipline but, more likely, by letting it be a time for sharing, listening, laughing, and enjoying each other. In fact, we may draw closer to God when milk can be spilled without anger and recrimination, when a child is free to pray what he feels and not by rote, and especially—would you believe—when your teenager *volunteers* to do the dishes.

O God, Help us not to cry over spilt milk. Forgive us when we practice bad table manners, but help us never to substitute manners for the realities of love for one another and for You. In the name of Him who transformed a simple meal of five loaves and two fishes into a celebration. Amen.

ON
THE
FAMILY
"DAWG"

In the annals of canine history, much has been written of the legendary feats by great dogs of the western world. Lassie, Rin Tin Tin, and others have captured the imagination of youth and adult alike, and the dog has come to be known as man's best friend.

Heretofore neglected, however, has been the child's best friend, the family dog or, more aptly named, "dawg." There is good reason for this neglect, of course, as such animals are well known for their insignificance. Family "dawgs" seldom have pure blood lines, although most come from good neighborhoods. Many merely attach themselves to families or "follow children home from school," especially if coaxed and bribed every step of the way.

Once established as part of the family, certain characteristics soon become apparent. For example, most—if not all—"dawgs" are neurotic and loaded with idiosyncrasies. A common one is the aversion to cleanliness, as such creatures will invariably head for the nearest dirt or manure pile immediately following that great adventure in frustration known as "washing the dog."

The canine creature who rules this writer's household has other peculiarities as well. She refuses to walk through puddles of water, and should she be out walking one of us on a leash, she will adamantly refuse to get her feet wet. The result is that her human companion will walk through or attempt to jump over a puddle, frequently with interesting consequences. Our "dawg" will bark late into the night if her feelings have been hurt. She refuses to sleep on a bare floor, insisting upon a rug or a mat before retiring for the night. She will accept bones only if they are thrown into the bushes, as she enjoys the adventure of foraging for them. This means we have not only a neurotic dog but also some of the sickest looking shrubs in town.

"Dawgs" are useless. Ours has been chasing the same squirrel up the same tree for years. They have been chasing and being chased for so long, in fact, that on hot summer days they walk through their routine. Nor do family dogs prove to be effective watchdogs. Should a burglar break into our house, Terry (an absurd name and therefore appropriate) would undoubtedly watch him steal the silver while begging him for a handout. The only person at whom she barks is the postman, who refuses to deliver our mail every now and then because he seems to be the only living creature afraid of the dog.

"Dawgs" are expensive, troublesome, and messy. They are usually inside when you want them out and outside when you want them in. They will refuse exotic dog food that makes its own gravy, then raid the neighbor's garbage can for left-over sauerkraut. In short, there is no good practical reason why families should keep a "dawg."

Of course, there is no good reason for having small children around either. They, too, are expensive, trying, time-consuming, and—at stages—not in complete control of their natural functions. From a "practical" point of view, dogs, children, the handicapped, the elderly, and many others do not merit their keep.

The reason, though, why we do keep them is that they are loved. The love of people for dogs, dogs for people, and some people for some other people is its own justification. It is enough to say "we love our dog," or "we love him."

Our task is to love those who are not "our own." When other people's "dawgs" bother us—indeed, when other people nag us, frustrate us, hurt us, make messes for us, and confound our existence—life will be intolerable unless we can include them in the scope of our love. If we can do so, we may then glimpse the magnificence of God's love for us, which pursues us like the Hound of Heaven, regardless of *our* merits.

O God, Keep us open to the lessons children and "dawgs" teach us. Forgive us for setting conditions on our love. In the Name of Him whose love embraced all Your creation. Amen.

ON
JOINING
INDIAN GUIDES

It is a known fact that practically no real Indians are members of the YMCA Indian Guide Program where a man can learn to be "pals forever" with his son. Evidently, they know something that middle-class fathers do not know, or perhaps those noble Americans have suffered enough.

For one thing, the men soon learn that a special language is used in all "tribal" meetings. Fathers are "Big Braves" and sons are always referred to as "Little Braves." In addition, each father and each son must take an Indian name, which is to be used at all times during the meetings; i.e., "Big Skunk and Little Skunk welcome Red Fox and Silver Fox to their teepee." Since business meetings are often conducted while sitting cross-legged on the floor, a newcomer to the tribe may want to enlist the aid of the medicine man or at least change his name to "Very Creaky Knees" or "Big Pain in the Groin."

If the language barrier is not sufficiently humiliating, the tribe soon learns it is to have craft projects for all the Little Braves. While the literature assures us that the Little Braves are to do the crafts, certain small doubts cross the mind as we learn that last year's tribe produced a twelve-foot-high, hand-carved, beautifully painted totem pole. Indeed, when the chief (usually a veteran) polls the Big Braves to see how many power saws and electric sanders are available to the group, we may even harbor the thought that the instruction manual speaks with forked tongue. Since some fathers are *not* handy with crafts, certain feelings of inferiority may turn Big Skunk into Chicken Little.

Subsequent meetings, however, prove that he does not really have an inferiority complex. They prove, instead, that he is inferior. Fathers not only have to master craftsmanship; they must also prove their virility over and over again, whether or not they have any. Camping out is one of the ways in which this is done. Some tribes have been known to hold winter campouts in which they pitch tents in the snow and build fires and sneeze a lot. Or the tribe may choose to have a Camp In, this being the experience of spending the night in a gymnasium, sleeping side by side with other big and little braves on blankets on top of a hardwood floor which was undoubtedly laid over six inches of poured concrete. No wonder Indians (at least pseudo-Indians) say "ugh" a lot.

Why, in the face of such dangers, do reasonably sane adult males of their own free will participate in such a program? They do so, surely, for many reasons, both good and bad. Mostly, however, they participate because they don't want to be simply "pals" with their sons; they want to be "fathers" to them.

It is comforting to note, in fact, that the Indian Guide manual does not take its own slogans *too* seriously. It quotes Dr. David B. Lynn as follows:

> The presence of the father seems especially important in the development of boys. The boy in effect says of his father, "So that is what it is like to be a man." If there is genuine love, the son will learn the subtleties of being a man without any special effort from the father. If this be true, the father is a better representative of manhood if he does not relegate his role to "just being a pal" to his son. The father should represent the adult male, not the boy's peer group. Usually the boy has plenty of "pals," but he has only one father.

If this be taken seriously, then father and son can relax and enjoy each other, both by being ridiculous at times and merely inept at others. The practice of Christian love expects this of all who follow the Master—even of awkward fathers and adolescent boys who speak in strange tongues and wear silly headbands for the sake of their relationship with one another.

O GREAT SPIRIT, Forgive us for so neglecting our sons that we feel guilty. Be with all Your people everywhere and at all times, and particularly during Indian Guide meetings. In His spirit, Amen.

ON
EATING AT
HAMBURGER
STANDS

The correlation between the population explosion and the abundance of hamburger stands in America is no accident. Kids who have become accustomed to men walking on the moon still light up with anticipation when modern man suggests to modern woman that they "grab a sandwich" for supper.

An 18¢ hamburger helps satisfy what must be a hereditary American craving for grease that exists in all children and most adults through age forty. Indeed, the fondness of children for cheap food is one of their more redeeming characteristics, even though many grow up without ever having to use a knife and fork in a public place.

It is well-known among parents, of course, that the

ability to enjoy cheap food is dependent upon several factors, not the least of which is whether or not it is edible. This writer has been sold, in the name of hamburger, a great variety of patties made from the chopped fiber of some unknown animal, possibly iguana. He has discovered that edibility is inversely proportional to the number of processes the food undergoes before being fried and to the length of time it remains in grease. The collective term for such sandwiches is "tango burgers," so-called because they dance in your stomach the whole night through. It is good advice to forego eating them, as they have a tendency to cause a great variety of abdominal pains.

One can have a modicum of confidence in his hamburgers if he sticks to the better-known places. Which restaurant he chooses, however, will depend less upon the juiciness of the burger than the popularity of the prize given away with each purchase. Thus, a family may find itself eating double cheeseburgers on Tuesday because that's the day a customer gets "free" Snoopy decals for pasting on a great number of inappropriate surfaces. It means that the same family may one day own a complete collection of Coke glasses by eating hamburgers in a restaurant where you get to keep the glasses, at least until they get broken on the way home.

One of the psychological dimensions of eating at hamburger places is "getting the order straight." Mistakes in placing one's order can lead to sibling rivalry—a sociological term meaning crying, screaming, and possibly getting sick all over the back seat. Unfortunately, mistakes are sometimes made by fathers and mothers. This occurs in proportion to the number of children concerned, especially when all express their desires simultaneously or when at least two of them insist upon items that are not for sale. Children also have been known to change their minds after the order has been placed, a fact which is one of the most convincing arguments for celibacy ever presented.

If the food is good and the order straight, the primary question that remains is: where do we eat the food? Eating in the car offers the special advantage to parents of being able to yell at the children when they spill their milk shakes without being heard by a restaurant full of onlookers. This must be weighed, however, against the alternative fact that dried milk shake that has oozed between the car seats stays with you for many trips to come.

Nevertheless, in the experience itself there is a message to be devoured. The significance of the event is neither in the quality of the food nor the uniqueness of the occasion. As closely as modern industrial processing can manage it, it will duplicate every other hamburger, milk shake, and French fry in the history of the firm. No surprises are planned, as quality is defined in terms of standardization and consistency.

We need to remember that anticipation of the familiar has its own kind of joy. The old hymns, favorite stories, the remembered smells from the kitchen, family traditions, old hangouts—reliving these is not simply sentimental silliness. They are part of the process of passing on customs, the warp and woof of tradition that bind generations together. Children of our children may look back at the visit to the hamburger stand with warm and pleasant memories, not very different from the way earlier generations remembered going to town on Saturday night. Thus, even the lowly hamburger has its symbolic value, as it reminds us that ground beef is part of the Ground of our Being together.

O LORD, Watch over the short-order cooks of the world. Help them to keep the grease traps clean and the milk shakes thick. Enable us to enjoy the familiar in life, as a child does, with satisfaction. In the name of Him who encouraged us to break bread together. Amen.

ON
GOING TO
DRIVE-IN
MOVIES

Parents should take their children to drive-in movies only after careful planning and intensive preparations. Part of what must be anticipated is the selection of the movie itself. Shows appropriate for family viewing are never rated anything other than "G". Even "PG" (Parental Guidance Suggested) is often misleading, as this standard is seemingly set with Ma Barker or the Marquis de Sade as the parents in mind. Walt Disney's productions are usually safe, and they aim for a mental audience of approximately the sixth grade —which is about right for those of us who plan to spend five hours in a car with small children.

Selecting the right movie, of course, does not mean that a family will be spared scenes of rape, incest, violence, and sadism. These ingredients are provided in the previews of coming attractions, as the juiciest parts of next week's offerings are lifted out and shown in front of your very eyes in vivid lurid-color. Such scenes do not go unnoticed by children who have been reprimanded for using a dirty word or discouraged by their parents from running naked through the neighborhood. Previews of "PG" rated films are not always edifying either, as many are like *Willard*, a movie about a young psychopath who trains rats to terrify and attack people. In such moments a policy of distraction sometimes works, as a parent can try to call attention to the beauties of nature—if there *are* any in a drive-in movie.

Even if previews prove to be relatively harmless, other problems must still be faced. Any family that contains small children will necessarily have to adjust to the lateness of the hour. Thus, some families fix a comfortable bed in the rear of the station wagon and take along a child's favorite pajamas, the ones with the pink rabbits chasing butterflies, in the hope that they will fall asleep and not have their growth stunted.

Unfortunately, drive-in movie owners manage to disrupt the best-laid plans of such conscientious but naïve parents. All outdoor theaters have playground equipment, which means that one's children can dash furiously from the car at an hour well past their normal bedtime to climb a rickety jungle gym while dressed in pajamas decorated with pink rabbits chasing butterflies.

At the last possible moment, precipitated by enraged parents honking their horns, the show begins. No, it doesn't. What begins is a series of animated cartoons, which is then followed by an "intermission," accompanied by large pictures on the screen of hamburgers, ice cream, and big orange drinks calculated to excite the salivary glands of any person less disciplined than St. Francis of Assisi. It is at approximately 10:00 P.M. that the family, well stuffed on overpriced food, settles down to watch the first full-length feature.

Wrong again! It is about this time that the problems of seeing the screen from the confines of an automobile become apparent. Father moves to the extreme left side of the car because the rear-view mirror blocks his vision. This causes his head to be in the way of his daughter who complains loudly and accidentally kicks over the big orange drink of her brother who was trying to see by balancing on the hump in the floor where the drive shaft is located. Mother gets out of the car to go to the back seat to help clean up the mess, forgetting that the speaker is attached to the door on her side. This oversight cracks the window glass and awakens the four-year-old who discovers she does not have her favorite stuffed animal and vows, loudly, never to sleep again.

All such occurrences are only the prelude, however, to the inevitable need of the children *in succession* to visit the bathroom. While it seems inconsistent that children who can risk their lives on a jungle gym and mingle with suspicious persons in a refreshment booth need parental help to visit a rest room, that is the way it is. It also helps explain why many adults consider the best part of the movie to be the words, "THE END," that appear on the screen at 1:30 A.M. and release the family from another happy and fun-filled evening of interpersonal relationships.

The drive-in movie, therefore, is one more testing ground

for the great American belief in "togetherness." As such, it is also an excellent place for families to try out the virtues of daily Christian living. Older children have opportunity to relate to younger ones—with responsibility. Huge amounts of physical touching occur, making the need for encounter group experiences unnecessary. In short, such occasions call the bluff—if it is a bluff—of those families who believe in patience, love, forgiveness, and responsibility. For what does it profit a family if it believes all the right things, but can't practice them in a station wagon well past bedtime?

O LORD, Forgive the movie-makers, theater managers, concession stand operators, and us for complicating a simple and potentially enjoyable event. Give us the good humor to enjoy modern entertainment and, if possible, grant us time for a nap the day after the night before at a drive-in movie. In the name of Him who taught us patience. Amen.

ON
STAYING IN
MOTELS

Americans are more mobile than ever before. They travel from sea to shining sea, looking for adventure or just trying to enjoy life away from home and crab grass. Those who have experienced such trips have also learned that they should not be entered into unadvisedly, but discreetly and in fear of God.

For one thing, there is the constant threat of getting lost. One needs to chart his course with care, and even then he is not safe, especially if his wife and children are reading the map and watching for road signs. Father-driver types are not particularly helped when, in response to the question "How far to the next town?" an eleven-year-old replies, "On the map it looks to be about an inch." Nor is one's peace of mind uplifted when a wife suggests we take a certain route because "it looks cute." Even more basic is the discovery that reading a map right side up keeps a car from going in exactly the opposite direction intended.

However, we must do more than plan our routes with care. We must be sure to anticipate that decision of decisions for weary travelers—where to spend the night. Contrary to popular opinion, motels are not owned and operated by near or distant relatives of Jesse James—some are under the care of persons related to the Mafia—but there are also inexpensive motels to be found.

"Inexpensive" may not properly modify the word "motel" in this instance, as the adjectives "cheap" and possibly "crummy" might be more appropriate. This writer stayed in one such establishment recently, and thereby learned to choose his words with care—as well as his motels in the future. The plumbing in this particular building made weird (but loud) noises for several minutes after the faucets were turned off, which wasn't all bad in that it drowned out the jukebox from the restaurant next door. The bed was clean and tidy, we can report, and most doctors agree that it is impossible to acquire curvature of the spine from spending one night in such a bed. Besides, we got up several times to rest.

Better accommodations are available at bigger prices, of course, and several large motel chains do not charge for children under twelve who stay in the same room with their parents. Obviously, very few parents who are in possession of their faculties would choose to stay in one room with four children, but necessity makes strained bedfellows—to coin a phrase. The end result in such circum-

35

stances is wall-to-wall wiggling, and parents can be sure that the night will seem long as children move from bed to bed, or take the most direct route to the bathroom, which is usually across a brother's or sister's stomach, and leading to what the sociologists call "familial conflict" and generals label "open warfare."

When we stay in expensive motels and still suffer, we are tempted to *get our money's worth* in whatever ways we can. We take showers when we're not dirty—because they're there. We pocket all the matchbooks when we neither smoke nor burn our trash. Shoeshine cloths are always used, and we deposit the extra little bars of soap in our suitcases and forget them until somebody notices we smell like Ivory Soap.

We watch color TV because it's free, and sit under the heat lamp in the bathroom when we'd rather go to bed, because something within us compels us to enjoy luxury we've paid for, whether we want it or not. We drink complimentary coffee when we don't normally drink coffee at all, and the ice bucket full of water from the melted ice we didn't use but scooped out of the machine—because it was there—greets us in the morning as a damp symbol of our dilemma.

In short, we find in luxury motels the temptation to "spiritual kleptomania"—the temptation to use things that are free to satisfy longings we don't have. Yet, the Christian faith reminds us to be good stewards, to live simply enough and wisely enough that we don't confuse basic needs with small indulgences. A sign that we've learned this lesson may be that time we're able to spend the night in a motel and *not* use all the towels just because they're there.

O God, As we travel across the land, help us to stay in motels we can afford and be grateful for the comfort they provide. Free us from wastefulness and help us not to complain or make inconveniences seem like problems. In the name of Him who traveled about doing good. Amen.

ON
TAKING
YOUR SON
TO A
BASEBALL GAME

Professional baseball continues to be the great American pastime. Critics of the game point out that it is slow-moving, at times colorless, and occasionally even tedious. The reason, fellow sports fans, why it is still supported by millions of people, in spite of its faults, is easily explained: all adult fans were once little boys who were taken to games by their fathers.

During the innocent years, when adult men try to be "good fathers" and their sons learn to take advantage of this weakness, baseball sometimes becomes a substitute for everything else, including household chores, education, and religion. Kids who bring home math papers from school with so much red on them they look as if they had bled to death can recite the batting averages of entire teams, from the biggest star down to the utility infielders. A boy who won't eat breakfast at all will suddenly be convinced that he will die within a week from malnutrition if Krispy Corn Kritters are not served for breakfast each morning for the next thousand years—a sure sign that Willie Mays says he eats them for breakfast, too.

Bubble gum cards become more important than money, for on them are pictures of baseball players. These will be carried in a boy's billfold and shown with great pride to neighborhood cronies, while pictures of mother, father, and Aunt Mildred (who hints that she may remember him in her will) are left behind. A boy who claims that carrying out the trash will cause a hernia will be able to play ball for six consecutive hours in a broiling sun with no apparent damage.

Such phenomena are not to be construed as evil, of course, and the above-named activities serve to keep boys out of poolrooms and other dens of iniquity. From the father's point of view, however, it is important that he know all the implications of such behavior patterns. It is especially important that he know the consequences of taking small boys to big league baseball games, an experience in together-ness that often leads—as the Bible says—to weeping and gnashing of teeth.

Most major league teams sponsor father-son nights wherein all boys under twelve get in free when accompanied by their fathers who pay double. This means that several thousand other fathers will accompany their sons to the same game, which results in a rather large crowd. The large crowd, in turn, causes the selection of seats for the game to be limited, and many fathers and sons are privileged to watch the game from high in the right field bleachers. Such a fate does promote healthy father-son dialogue, however, as the father gets to explain that there really are nine men on a team even though they can only see seven from where they are sitting.

To help assuage anxiety and encourage joy among the boys, fathers often purchase refreshments for their sons. It is during this time that they learn the real reason why boys attend sporting events: they go to eat. Their strange adolescent appetites crave foot-long hot dogs, ice cream bars, salted peanuts, and four-ounce cups of lemonade made from a large amount of water, a small amount of sugar, and one antique lemon. All this must be bought from vendors who, after years of practice, know precisely where to stand in order to block one's vision of the game. Each item, of course, must be passed from person to person until, miraculously, it gets to the child who ordered it, after which the money is passed back to the vendor in the same fashion, the change returned, and the whole process repeated because the kids of the father two seats to your right now want some, too.

In the meantime the home team has scored twice; there have been two errors and a triple play; and a Coke has been spilled on your left foot. Within fifteen minutes of these events, fathers will start the process of accompanying their sons to the rest room, as small boys on an average go to the bathroom every other inning. Even if only brief periods of time are used in responding to Nature's call, they will undoubtedly be crucial ones to the outcome of the game. Indeed, there is nothing quite so disconcerting to an adult baseball fan as to be fumbling for money for a pay toilet while listening to the roar of the crowd outside.

The message in all this is obvious. If a father takes his young son to a baseball game in the name of bettering their relationship, he must be willing to pay the price. If he is going because *he* likes baseball and his son is an excuse, he is probably going to encourage apartness, not togetherness. If, knowing this, he still goes to the game with his son, much good can be accomplished. The boy will brag to his friends for days about the trip, and the dad can read the newspaper the next day and find out what happened at the game. The hard hat, the miniature bat, and the team pennant he brought home from the ball park will justify a boy's upset stomach, and his father will be relieved of a few guilt feelings he had been having for not spending enough time with his son.

It may even be that the peripheral events of the experience are *more* important than watching the game itself. To *share* the experience of planning for, answering questions about, and taking sons to the game may be more spiritually enriching than silently watching other people performing on a distant playground. Taking a small boy to a baseball game keeps it from being merely a spectator sport, and baseball—like the Christian religion—is only joyful when it is experienced rather than observed from afar.

O GOD, Watch over all fathers and sons who go to baseball games. Be close to the vendors, ticket salesmen, and ushers who hold the keys to the enjoyment of the game in their hands. In the name of Him who was with You in the big-inning. Amen.

ON
TEENAGE
MUSIC

When parents discover that their children want a record player for Christmas, they can be sure a new phase of adolescence has begun. Given the influence of the media and the awesome power of peer group pressure, teenagers will necessarily observe their own tribal rites of initiation by buying, playing, replaying, loaning, discussing, and dancing to phonograph records, some of which have words and music. The main difference between these rites, however, and those more sensible ones observed by jungle natives is that parents suffer through them as well.

It is an unwritten rule that records are always played with the volume at maximum output, as this enables hapless neighbors within a ten-block range to share the experience whether they want to or not. Paradoxically, the loudness of the music causes the words of the songs to be blurred, whereas a softer tone enables us to understand the words and discover that, in fact, the *meanings* are blurred.

While the following example will not be popular by the time you read these words, other songs just as obtuse will surely be sweeping the country to support the above contention. Consider, if you dare, the following verbal expressions contained in a popular classic* that has received a three-aspirin rating from the author and his wife:

Wee de de de, de de de de de wee
Un bum ba way! (Repeat)
Aheya aha wenowit wenowit
Awamawit awemawit awemawit awemawit (Repeat)
In the jungle, the mighty jungle, the lion sleeps tonight.
In the jungle, the quiet jungle, the lion sleeps tonight.
Aka, aka, heeeeeeee de de de de wedo, umbedo um ba way
(Repeat)

Other lyrics, equally moving, are part of this song, but perhaps these will sufficiently illustrate the point without explaining how a lion, or anybody else, could sleep with all that racket.

To be fair to teenage music, which is difficult under the circumstances, some of the songs show a highly developed social conscience. This is because the performers and the writers of the music are continually looking for material aimed at anticapitalist youth, since that's where the money is. It is difficult, however, to take musical performers seriously when they claim to reject the past, especially when they have so many Daniel Boone haircuts, Mark Twain mustaches, and Abe Lincoln beards.

*"The Lion Sleeps Tonight," © Folkways Music Publishers, Inc.

Some songs are played primarily for their beat and rhythm, and to these, teenagers vigorously dance. It does not resemble, of course, "real" dancing (translation: our kind) which, our guardians used to remind us, was a "perpendicular expression of a horizontal desire." Instead, it consists of doing a variety of calisthenics to music, without touching a partner at all and many times without any awareness that other human beings are even present. Other than a genuine threat of universal deafness from the music, teenage dancing may be the biggest boon to physical fitness since Joseph invented tennis by serving in Pharaoh's court.

The temptation for parents to be afraid of youth culture, particularly their music, is real, just as the pioneers were afraid of the Indians because of their strange appearance and odd noises. True, some of the names of the musical groups are scary, and it is unnerving to realize your beloved children are off in a corner listening to The Grateful Dead or Three Dog Night. Nonetheless, to expect them to enjoy Lawrence Welk or Guy Lombardo is to expect too much.

Probably it will be best to let them have their music, albeit with the volume turned down, and argue about bigger issues. One way to get high blood pressure is to go mountain-climbing over molehills, and teenage music is not really sinister, only strange. Paul Tournier reminds us: "An emotional bond is established between those who know the same secret which they agree to hide from everyone else." It may *not* be our right to know teenage secrets, even the secret language and meaning of their music. To accept them *with* their secrets—this is understanding.

It is to *understanding* that we, as adults, are called, if we can hear the call above the sound of that awful music.

O FATHER, Help us not to pry where we have no right, so that our children may delight in their secrets. Give us healthy eardrums and a forgiving spirit. Most of all, please don't remind us of the silly music of our youth. In the name of Him who, like us, needed silence occasionally. Amen.

ON
PUTTING
CHILDREN
TO BED AT NIGHT

There are many excellent theories on how to get children to go to bed at night. Some of them work, although not often. There is a natural resistance in children to going to bed at night akin to the natural immunity they have toward certain diseases. Indeed, most children regard going to bed as comparable to having a disease, as they simply will not recognize the fact that they need their sleep so that parents can get some rest.

So, the competition begins each evening with parents on one side and the products of their family planning on the other. Usually, parents employ a twofold strategy of Rewards and Punishments, or, "Speak softly but wear a big frown." The father or the mother will say, "Let's go up and get into our 'jammies' and I'll read you a story." The children will counter with, "May we have a snack first?"

This, of course, is the opening move in the children's game plan, usually known as The Big Stall. Night after night, parents who had to play games with a four-year-old to get her to eat her potatoes at dinner ("Pretend this bite is the airplane and your little mouth is the hangar") will be treated to a scene of food consumption comparable only to the training table of the Green Bay Packers. They will watch as a kid who's finished many a dinner with more food on his plate than when he began downs a bowl of cereal, two glasses of milk, and a peanut butter sandwich— very, very slowly.

Knowing that full stomachs lead to drowsiness, the parents think privately to themselves that they are going to win the war even though they've lost the first battle. The children, however, are merely preparing for Phase II, herein identified as The Bathroom Ritual in which children are to concern themselves with washing of faces, brushing of teeth, and lower anatomical needs. It is reasonable to suppose that all such matters could take place during one visit to the bathroom, but reason has little to do with it, and one can be certain that several trips back and forth will have to be made before the final toothbrush will be left, dripping, to hang for the night.

It is about this time that parents apply the Firmness theory. This usually consists of strongly worded ultimatums, such as "Now I mean it" or "Get to bed or else." Such declarations work best if they are uttered through clenched teeth and if the parent is never forced to answer the question, "Or else, *what?*" Firm ultimatums are good exercise for the facial muscles, as well as providing one's children with private reactions of amusement.

Once in bed, the children will undoubtedly help the parent remember that a story has been promised, an event which promotes considerable discussion as to selection and length. Whatever is the final choice, there is usually little need for it to be read at all, as the kids know most of it by heart. The parent discovers this when he tries to short-cut the whole experience by skipping a few pages, only to have his kids rise straight up in bed in righteous indignation and issue loud calls for the *whole* story.

By this time the children will have begun to tire of the game somewhat, especially since they have won. Only a few sporadic incidents will take place, such as a request for another drink or the discovery that a favorite stuffed animal is missing, without which a child will be psychologically damaged for life. These are usually only brief encounters, however, and the armistice is near at hand.

When the children are finally in bed, all safe and sound-less, many parents are able to understand why younger and stronger adults are the ones whom God designated to be parents. On many nights, however, they may also experience a quality of relationship that Christians call agape love. As a parent gazes down on his child sleeping in a bed so filled with stuffed animals, books, and favorite things that his head rests on the window sill and his right leg is wrapped around a bedpost, he may feel a joy unspeakable.

Bedtime is more than a time to go to bed. It is a time for making things right, for the scratching of backs and saying of prayers, for kissing and hugging and vowing an important promise: "We'll see you in the morning."

If there's enough love and sufficient tenderness, putting children to bed at night may be the only battle in the world where everybody wins.

> As we lay them down to sleep,
> We pray Thee, Lord, their souls to keep.
> If they wake up before they should,
> We pray Thee, Lord, help them be good.
> In the name of Him who slept in a manger.
>   Amen.

ON
SHOPPING
FOR YOUR
WIFE

As chauvinistic as it sounds, most married men are convinced that shopping is a characteristic as inherently female as having babies. In fact, the analogy between having babies and going shopping is, if you'll pardon the expression, a pregnant one; i.e., a man can participate in the enterprise but he can never produce the results a woman can.

For one thing, he simply does not have the stamina. He may exercise regularly at the YMCA, jog two miles each evening, and chin himself twelve times before breakfast. Nevertheless, an afternoon of shopping with his wife will leave him with sore legs, a migraine headache, and a degree of fatigue first noticed in military personnel who survived the Bataan Death March in World War II. His weariness, of course, is partly psychological, as men naïvely think their purchases can be made when they've found that for which they have been shopping. Not so, if a wife is along. Once found, that article must then be compared for price, quality, and condition in every other store within a two-mile radius. A man will pay $2.00 for a $1.00 item he wants, but a woman can't be sure she wants it until she is convinced it is the best buy in town.

At Christmas, however, husbands are on their own. To buy or not to buy is scarcely the question. What to buy becomes the issue. So intimidated has he become from past shopping excursions with his wife, the average husband has little confidence in his taste or selective abilities. He knows that she wears a size 12 dress, unless it is in an expensive line, in which case she can wear a 10, or occasionally an 8 in certain styles. Even if he lucks out on the dress size, he is uncertain about length, for if he gets one that is too short, it won't look right, and if it's too long, she'll think he regards her as dowdy.

What he'd really like to get her is some red lingerie, partly because red goes with Christmas, and partly because the mental image of his wife in red underwear causes his juices, and hopefully hers, to flow faster. However, for most middle-aged men who have not been completely liberated from their sexual hang-ups, the process of purchasing bras and panties from a young female clerk has its own built-in stays (if, once again, you'll pardon the pun).

In the first place, all clerks who sell lingerie have no inhibitions whatsoever and positively delight in humiliating the male customers. "What size cup would you like?" she asks, knowing full well he doesn't know, while he finds it suddenly impossible to approximate the size without using his hands. "Would you like a 'cross-your-heart' or a 'divide-and-conquer' style?" she inquires rather loudly, it seems, when by that time he would happily settle for a black gunnysack with pink elastic just to escape.

Such clerks are not easily dissuaded, however, and they will quickly interpret the ridiculous expression on his face as sales resistance. "Here, just feel the material," she may say as she thrusts a tiny pair of pink panties into his hands, while he, feeling like an escaped sex maniac, tries not to notice the other customers who have stopped to stare. By this time he is mumbling incoherently and perspiring, which enables him to escape further humiliation because the sales-girl has begun to think perhaps he is, in fact, a sex maniac.

Such experiences explain why so many wives are given books, toasters, ironing boards, and gift certificates for Christmas. In fact, these words are being written to assure wives all over America that the gift of an electric can opener does not mean a lack of love, but of courage. Nor does a carpet sweeper indicate that romance has gone out of a marriage. It probably means that carpet sweepers are sold next to lingerie departments in some stores, and many traumatized husbands would have given their wives boa constrictors had that department provided an escape route from lingerie clerks.

Whatever anxiety is produced will make little difference in the long run to people who have been married fifteen years or more. Husbands who love their wives will try to find ways of saying it with gifts at Christmas. Wives who love their husbands will rejoice in whatever he brings, whether or not it fits and regardless of cost—especially if he saves the sales slips.

O LORD, Grant us courage for the living of these days, especially around Christmas. Forgive all aggressive clerks as well as inept husbands. In the name of Him whose birth started the whole thing. Amen.

ON
SEX,
FIFTEEN YEARS
LATER

Never before in the history of American society have so many talked so freely so often about sex as now. Indeed, if practice is related to any degree with preaching about sex, it has probably already replaced basketball as our leading indoor sport.

Literature on the subject ranges from heavy, scholarly essays to bad, old-fashioned pornography which has moved from the sewer to the newsstand. All of this material can be very threatening to those of us who were married fifteen years ago, believe it or not, as virgins. While then we regarded our way as both normal and virtuous, today we wonder if anyone under thirty would give us a hearing—if, indeed, we were to do any talking, which we do little of when it comes to sex because of our inhibitions, our Puritanism, and the fact that it's nobody's business but our own.

Yet, since every third magazine carries an article about wife-swapping or communal living or trial marriages or new forms of sexual experimentation, we wonder if we have missed something. As in Robert Frost's poem, "the road not taken" may have made a big difference, for our sexual beginnings in marriage surely seem different from what we read today.

Certainly many modern couples are starting out with more sophistication and poise when it comes to sex than we did. Looking back from the vantage point of the fifteenth wedding anniversary, this writer's wife was about as poised as Little Orphan Annie and he probably presented himself to his new bride as a Gomer Pyle of the bedroom—eager but terribly awkward.

This is not to say that it was easy to arrive at one's wedding night as a virgin. It is reasonable to assume that one's sexual drives were as strong then as they are for young people today, and there were lots of things we wanted to know about sex but were afraid to ask. In those days before the pill and with no Playboy Advisor to guide us, we lived under the fear of Consequences and a Moral Code that, in its more extreme forms, hinted that white marks on our fingernails were the direct result of evil thoughts. Even so, opportunities were available to creative couples, and virginity was preserved only by intense moral striving and many laps around the track followed by cold showers.

Was it worth it? Who can really know, as some virgins who got married also got divorced, and expressed their passions in the meantime primarily by hating their spouses.

Others who were, shall we say, "more experienced" seemingly have lived happily ever after. We can't really say which kind of sexual beginning produces the best results, for the measurement of such matters is, at best, imprecise.

What we can do is give our own testimony on sex, fifteen years later. We can say that sex has been an important part of our lives, as it has helped us experience considerable happiness and fulfillment. Let us even suggest that there have been many memorable nights of sexual union—the kind the movies record with stereophonic music and in technicolor. Not the least of these was the occasion when the bed slats broke on our first night in a new home.

We have learned, also, to laugh about our sex lives, to laugh even about our awkward beginnings and about those nights when my brother telephoned at highly inappropriate times. We continue to share our favorite sex jokes over and over again, and they never cease to be funny because they are part of our having learned to laugh at sex together. (E.g.: *She.* [*Sighing.*] "I can't believe we're finally married." *He.* [*In a voice of utter frustration.*] "You'll sure know it as soon as I can get this darn shoelace untied!")

The bed, for people married fifteen years, becomes a symbol of life together. To go to bed is to go to bed *together*, even though each is perfectly capable of getting ready by himself and turning back the covers without help. To go to bed is to make peace with one another, for to sleep together while angry is a contradiction in terms.

At times we allow ourselves the arrogant thought that we may know more about sex than Hugh Hefner, Elizabeth Taylor, and other world leaders. Certainly we feel confident that we *know* each other in the Old Testament sense, for when the book of Genesis said that Abraham went in to Sarah and *knew* her, the sexual implications of that visit were obvious, even in the King James Version.

Since it seems clear that we can't take both sexual roads in the same lifetime, we happily affirm the road we have taken. We have discovered that making love is better than merely having sex, and people married fifteen years still tingle a little at the thought—and even more at the deed.

CREATOR GOD, Thank you for the gift of sex and for the coincidences of life which have allowed many of us to share the discovery of it exclusively with one other person. About this part of life, O God, we have no complaints. In the name of Him who blessed marriage at Cana of Galilee. Amen.

ON
JOINING
THE PTA
(ALAS!)

T he Apostle Paul wrote: "I do not even acknowledge my own actions as mine, for what I do is not what I want to do, but what I detest" (Romans 7:16, NEB). Contrary to what many Americans may think, Paul had not just returned from a PTA meeting, even though few organizations in the history of man have captured more time from more people with less enthusiasm than Parent-Teacher Associations.

If a secret and scientific poll could be taken to discover the real feelings of the several million parents and the seven or eight teachers who participate in such associations, a degree of apathy would probably be noted which would make Rip Van Winkle a social revolutionary by comparison. This is not to say that Parent-Teacher Associations fail to be busy. They sponsor chili suppers, ice cream socials, cake sales, and many interesting meetings. More precisely, a *small group* of members with masochistic tendencies, called officers, sponsor such events.

It is here, in fact, that the paradox of the above situation becomes clear. PTA officers, *in behalf of* an entire association, promote a large number of events, the response to which ranges from mild boredom to passionate indifference. Since the author's wife has been a PTA officer, a situation which might have led to divorce had she been home often enough to be served a court order, this apathetic reaction should restore our faith in democracy. A people who ignore PTA meetings can't be all bad.

Please do not misunderstand. The idea behind the organization is good, the intentions of the officers are excellent, and the dedication of many persons involved makes Shadrach, Meshach, and Abednego appear wishy-washy. However, the main burden the PTA carries is that it comes too late, with too much. It is regarded by the worn-out middle class as Just One More Thing. It is too much like membership in churches, lodges, and service clubs; and those organizations have prior claim on the guilt feelings needed to stimulate interest in Good Causes.

Since PTAs are for Better Education and Better Parent-Teacher Relationships, the average member will seldom say anything aloud in criticism. Privately, however, he may wonder what the link is between so many ice cream socials and Education; especially since the proceeds almost always go toward the purchase of new doors for the girls' toilets, or similar teaching equipment.

Indeed, if the secret were out, the officers wonder the

same thing. They are the ones, after all, who place eighty-five phone calls to recruit three women to serve refreshments at the next meeting which will be attended by the executive committee, the principal (who's paid to be there), and a guest speaker who will leave, if he has any sense, before the business meeting. They are also the ones who bake two cakes, four dozen cookies, and a pie apiece for a food sale; transport them to the school where they work three-hour shifts as salespersons; and conclude their evening by buying back stale sweet rolls and leftover doughnuts so the association can show a profit.

Somewhere in America, of course there are PTAs whose practices are closer to their purposes; and we have met, in person, individuals who are willing to shed blood for the next ice cream social. Good for them and for all others who like bloody ice cream! Nevertheless, for many veteran parents, the organization will stand as a continuing example of an abiding frustration of responsible selfhood—the gap between means and ends.

The famous statement, "Where there is no vision, the people perish," comes close to our dilemma, but in the case of the PTA it can be changed to read: "Where there is vision, but no way to reach it, the people think up excuses for not getting involved." Still, in this adventure, as in all of life, there is hope. After all, our children will eventually leave grade school, the PTA will become a part of a nostalgic memory, and a wonderful case for small families will have been made—especially with those who are descendants of PTA executive committees.

O LORD, We thank you for the dedication of the people

who work in PTA. We know Your power can redeem organizations, so please forgive our grumbling about the PTA, and help the next meeting to be better. If it isn't, grant us a valid excuse for missing. In the name of Him who knows our needs before we say them. Amen.

ON
READING
OLD
MAGAZINES

Of all the pleasures known to mankind, one of the most frequently overlooked is the reading of old magazines. It is a pleasure discovered, usually, on a dreary weekend when one decides to clean the garage or goes up to the attic to look for the ice cream freezer which has been put away in such a safe place it may never be found. Almost before he knows it, he is seduced by the cover of *Life*, or he can't resist the lead article in *Esquire* which, three years later, seems too interesting to ignore—as it was when the magazine appeared.

Such were the circumstances confronting this writer not long ago, and the experience of reading old magazines proved to be both delightful and—how shall we put it— "instructive."

It was a special treat to read the short stories, articles and epigrams of old *Saturday Evening Post*s, now gone forever. What irony to read the predictions of *January* that were foolish in June! Dusty copies of *Reader's Digest* provided more than enough old jokes to cause all one's neighbors with bad memories to regard him as a witty fellow.

Then came the big mistake. Quite by accident we started a continued *Post* story that began in early February. It was a typical whodunit, and it took all the February issues to get the crimes committed, most of March to provide suspects, the final March issue for the hero to realize he loved the gal, and the April 2 issue to lead us to the dénouement, the unraveling when all becomes clear. But, unfortunately, the concluding installment couldn't be found. April 9, 1960, either didn't exist or had been canceled.

A search revealed one *Harper's Bazaar*, a whole stack of *National Geographic*s, and a Sunday supplement to an ancient issue of *The Indianapolis Star*. The attic, the basement, the garage—all were searched and all, as the Bible says, were found lacking. April 16 was present and accounted for, May was easily located, even the Christmas issues from a previous year were there. However, April 9 was gone forever and with it the plot, the ending, the identity of the bad guys, and the concluding romance. Because there was no ending, the beginning and the middle were spoiled.

Something like this often happens to us in our daily lives, too. Much of the time our Christian experience seems exciting and relevant. We return from summer vacation, and church attendance is good and morale is high. We are rested and refreshed, and we look forward to our regular routines. We may go on a retreat and replan our lives, or set goals for ourselves and our churches which, on paper, have a good chance of bringing the Kingdom of God into being by Easter for sure, and possibly even by Groundhog Day.

Yet, if the projects we begin are not completed, or if initial dedication is not channeled into useful work, frustration replaces excitement, lethargy consumes energy, and that familiar road is resurfaced with good intentions. This is why people who like to describe themselves as "seekers" will remain frustrated if they do not, at some level, become "finders."

Life is a pilgrimage, to be sure, and we never know for certain where it will lead us. Nevertheless, life is also lived in chapters, each having a beginning, a middle, and an end. To live our lives without finishing what we start is to become dusty and incomplete—stored away where sunlight is scarce and pleasure comes only from reminiscing about what might have been.

O LORD, Help us to seek *and* to find, to start *and* to complete; so that we can see direction and purpose in our lives. Keep us contemporary and up to date, so we won't seem too much at home when we read old magazines in dusty attics. In the name of Him who warned us against the dangers of storing up treasures. Amen.

ON
WATCHING
TELEVISION

TV or not TV" is a question which rages from time to time in our homes. Since there are more than 100 million television sets in the United States, with 95 percent of our homes having at least one and many two TVs, there is potential for considerable raging.

Part of the problem is that families disagree among themselves as to which programs are appropriate for watching. Wives have strong feelings about what programs husbands should or should not watch, and vice versa. It is not unknown, for example, for some wives to be mildly critical of the time many husbands spend over weekends from September to January watching football. One may even glimpse a dab of family tension when a wife says, sweetly, as her husband emerges from the den after six hours of Sunday football games: "Children, see that nice man blinking his eyes from exposure to the light—that's your father; go show him how much you've grown!" One woman in Ohio even submitted a bill to the state legislature requesting the right of a wife to have her husband declared legally dead if he watched more than six hours of football on any given weekend.

Husbands, too, have used television as the scapegoat for other household frustrations. Upon discovering a shirt with missing buttons, the man of the house may inquire, more loudly than necessary, "Did you enjoy the afternoon shows today, dear?" Questions like this do very little to bind their marital union more firmly and may lead to cold cuts for dinner.

Perhaps the greatest difference of opinion centering on television, however, has to do with its effect on children. The temptation to use the tube as an electronic baby-sitter is a real one, and there are just enough "good" shows for children to allow parents some justification for the time their three- and four-year-olds sit in front of the box. After all, "Captain Kangaroo," "Sesame Street," and Dr. Seuss cartoons are their own excuse for being, and they have the additional advantage of keeping children located in the one place of which parents heartily approve—elsewhere!

The dilemma comes, however, when a three-year-old who doesn't know his ABCs can sing a beer commercial from beginning to end, with feeling. Maybe "Sesame Street" hasn't been the *only* program the kids have watched! If, as the analysts tell us, many preschool children, ages three to five, watch television an average of fifty-four hours per week, there is reason to believe that they will, indeed, grow into adulthood with poor eyesight and broad-beamed bottoms.

Thus, the father who arranges his life around crucial third-down situations all fall, and the mother who seeks romance in "Secret Storm" each weekday afternoon, are probably not going to monitor their children's TV habits with diligence. Instead, they (we?) will either feel guilty about the whole situation and do nothing about it, or sell the set to the next-door neighbors and let them feel guilty.

What's a family to do? Almost everything about television the sociologists tell us is true, and most of that is bad. Adults and children both watch too much television, which means too much violence, too much trivia, and too many snacks during commercials. Some of us will spend nearly ten years of our lives in front of a television screen, second only to the time we spend sleeping.

Furthermore, the primary purpose of the enterprise is to hold the attention of the audience long enough for it to be exposed to the commercial. Television at its worst is an effort to treat people as consumers, not as whole persons. It is primarily in the business of selling viewers to advertisers.

Chances are, we'll keep our sets, live with our guilt feelings, and resolve to do a better job of monitoring what our children view and how much time we ourselves are willing to give to Cyclops. The television dilemma, though, is an excellent modern example of a long-standing Christian problem; for in this area of life we can see clearly that *not to decide is to decide.*

Not to take a discriminating attitude toward television programing is to let Madison Avenue hucksters and Hollywood TV bureaucrats shape our values and direct our lives. Life is a series of choices about how we spend our time and the goals to which we commit ourselves. Television is getting a big hunk of this life, so we had better be sure we are running it and it is not running us.

Television watching must be a matter of conscious and conscientious decision-making, not the result of a blind faith that somehow everything will turn out all right. That happens only on the late, late shows.

O GOD, Guide us in our choices. Help us to not believe all that we see on TV, and to watch it less than we do. Encourage us to talk to each other and share real life together. Save us from the clutches of Big Eye. In the name of Him who taught us to seek first the Kingdom of God. Amen.

ON
TEACHING
SUNDAY SCHOOL

Critics have called it "the most wasted hour of the week," parents have entrusted the responsibility for moral and spiritual values to it, and children can't wait to outgrow it so they can become parents who will entrust moral and spiritual education to it. No one, however, can evaluate the Sunday school quite like that modern-day martyr, the would-be lion frequently eaten alive by Christians—the Sunday school teacher.

In one hour per week—minus time out for "opening exercises," a discussion of last night's basketball game, and a series of appeals (usually ignored) for quiet—the teacher is to bring up children in the way they should go. After a few attempts at teaching Sunday school, most teachers have some deeply held feelings about where at least some students should go, the choices ranging between federal prison and forced labor in a South American jungle.

The teacher, in short, discovers that his role is understood by many to be that of a disciplinarian. Thus, he is faced early in his career with the problem of expelling the worst trouble-makers from his class in order to teach the others about the unconditional love of God. His teachers' manual says that "each person is an individual with different potentialities and abilities, that each person is valuable for these separate capabilities, and that there is value in difference as well as in conformity." He concludes, however, that this really means all the kids are to make clay bunnies at the first sign of trouble.

Sunday school teachers, especially those working with the primary grades, may at times wonder if they are teaching Christianity or a junior version of *Popular Mechanics*. Surrounded by a clutter of paper-mâché, finger paints, Silly Putty, and left-over lumber from somebody's workbench, only the Sunday school teacher can know the terror which lies behind the childlike need to "take something home to mommy."

Object lessons are very important in Sunday school, too, although the connection between the object taught and the lesson learned is not always apparent. There is no doubt that drowning a worm in a glass of alcohol holds the attention of children, but it is disconcerting when the students conclude that the best way to get rid of worms is to drink alcohol.

There is, of course, no guaranteed way to teach children

what we want them to learn in Sunday school. Kids have a way of drawing their own conclusions, whether we drown worms, make clay bunnies, or force them to memorize Bible verses. If we "get back to the Bible" and use pictures of the twelve-year-old Jesus teaching in the temple, chances are at least one third-grader will conclude that Jesus, as pictured, was either a young girl with long hair who wore a bathrobe to church, or a very baby-faced boy who looked like a hippie. This, it is safe to say, is *not* what most parents want their children to believe about Jesus.

Given the special dilemmas the task of Sunday school teaching presents, why do otherwise intelligent and stable Christian people even try? The answer, like the enterprise itself, is unclear, other than the fact that not all people are as sane as they seem. It is important to note, however, that when famous adults are asked to name people who greatly influenced their lives, Sunday school teachers are among those most frequently mentioned. Even more noteworthy is that these teachers so favorably mentioned run the gamut of "types"—from little old ladies in high buttoned shoes to virile masculine types in sandals, from Bible-verse memorizers to clay bunny modelers.

Somehow, some way, the Christian faith was "caught," if not taught, from these persons. If this be true, it remains important to make Sunday school as intelligent and worthwhile as possible; but it is even more important that teachers of children have an infectious faith which is lived out in daily experience. And while such persons are always in demand, many of them surely must be teaching Sunday school, for that task requires the faith of Abraham and the courage of Daniel.

O God, Help us to suffer little children when they come to us during Sunday school. Open our minds to the best teaching methods available, but help us to be faithful to children by being faithful to You. In the name of Him who bugged His synagogue teachers. Amen.

ON
GIVING
DEVOTIONS

In the life span of nearly every Christian, whatever his degree of backsliddenness, will come the inevitable invitation to give devotions. Public meeting or private gathering, secular event or sacred occasion, church service or horse show—the Law and the Prophets decree that someone must give devotions.

Public devotions fall into certain categories. There are "instant devotions," sometimes called "God will lead the way." Such devotional meditations will be characterized by no preparation whatsoever, as the leader will simply flip open a Bible and, as they say in the theater, "wing it." Unfortunately, the listeners to such presentations often "wing it" too, as their minds fly to distant psychological shores.

A second category can be identified as "ultra-traditional" or "the little old church in the wildwood" syndrome. This is perhaps the most widely used type of devotion and leans heavily on back copies of the *Upper Room*, the farther back the better. Couched in the language of Zion, these devotionals sound the way devotions are supposed to sound, and the listeners will depart the meeting with peace of mind, knowing that holy language has been used even though they can't remember what was said.

Frequent devotion-givers often fall into a third category which is aptly described as the "TV dinner" variety. This means that the leader steals his material from somebody else's book and simply warms it up for public consumption. Relying on a source unfamiliar to the laity, such as *The Pastor's Friend* or *999 Stories to Warm the Heart By*, the leader attempts to breathe life into dry bones by introducing the material with phrases such as "a funny thing happened to me on the way to the church." Such devotions as these are almost always harmless, thereby meeting the primary test of appropriateness for both sacred and secular occasions.

A popular kind of devotional in recent years has been the "avant-garde" meditation, sometimes called "nouveau blah." College teachers and preachers hoping for honorary doctorates exemplify this category. The key to this type is a dependence upon French existentialist writers, such as Camus and Sartre. What these givers of devotions say is much less important than whether or not they pronounce French names properly. Avant-garde types utter such inclusive phrases as, "You are undoubtedly familiar with the helpful words of Descartes . . . ," to which their audiences respond by smiling and nodding, even though most of them think the leader is referring to a Canadian hockey player he saw on TV the night before.

Another contemporary type is represented by the "liturgical litany boys." These persons always pass out stained mimeographed sheets of paper for reading and response. While the intention—to involve the audience—is a noble one, almost always these leaders pick out the best parts for themselves. They usually read a long, sonorous part, to which everyone else is to reply, "Yea, verily." Sometimes the liturgy is written in the vernacular, however, and the expected response is changed to "You can say that again, Charlie . . ."—and he usually does.

A final category is the "Teutonic school" of devotions, characterized by totally incomprehensible content and numerous references to German theologians and their favorite phrases. The leader speaks of "Angst" and "Heilsgeschichte" and quotes Barth and Bonhoeffer as often as possible, usually with a certain tremolo in his voice. Such devotions are very helpful, as the audience feels profound without knowing why.

To whatever school we belong, however, we still share a common dilemma. How do we worship Almighty God in Spirit and Truth? How, with authenticity, does the creature approach the Creator? Our gimmicks, our intelligence, our clever efforts to bring about "worship"—all are found wanting much of the time. We find ourselves relearning what the Psalmist taught us many devotions ago: "The sacrifice acceptable to God is a broken spirit; a broken and contrite heart, O God, thou wilt not despise" (Ps. 51:17, RSV). This kind of devotion can be identified by a sense of awe, wonder, and the presence of God in the midst. It is beyond categories, for it is the Real Thing.

O God, Help us to be still and know You are God. Be present when we give devotions, for without You they seem rather contrived. In the name of Him who taught us how to pray. Amen.

ON
TRUSTING
MECHANICAL
THINGS

A friend of ours recently bought a transistor radio. As often happens, he had been convinced by newspaper advertisements that such radios are ideal companions. You can take them anywhere—to the beach, in the car, on the tennis court, or to football games. You may have seen the ad in which a lovely blonde girl and a handsome man are driving along in a convertible with a transistor between them, smiling contentedly as they listen to Tchaikovsky's Second Piano Concerto in B flat minor.

On the basis of such hopes, therefore, our friend bought one to use in the car, on the beach, and at football games. However, upon bringing it home from the store, he discovered it evidently wouldn't work anyplace else, such as in the living room of his home. It would stop playing at very illogical times for no apparent reason, usually right in the middle of somebody's cadenza.

There is perhaps no one in the world who dislikes an interrupted cadenza more than our music-loving friend, so he experimented at trying to get the radio started again. He installed new batteries, but the radio continued to sputter and squawk. By tapping it lightly with the index finger of the right hand, he discovered it would play for about ten minutes and then stop. Additional taps would start it, but often the music or news would come from a different station.

Eventually, he did what most patient and domesticated Americans do under such circumstances: he returned to the store where he had bought the radio and explained his problem—loudly. Was there a guarantee? The clerk informed him that the radio was fully and unconditionally guaranteed, except for parts and labor!

Undaunted, our friend proposed to demonstrate the frailties of the radio. He turned it on and confidently waited for it to sputter and die. It played happily. After a moment's waiting, he "encouraged" the short circuit by a gentle tap with the right index finger. It continued to play. He then hit it with his fist. It continued to play. Within five minutes he was pounding it on the desk with great force—an act which, if anything, made the tone quality even better.

The clerk behind the desk smiled politely, suggested that our friend bring the radio back "if the trouble continued," and gave him a look which indicated he thought all the loose screws were not in the transistor. Thus ended the tale of another victim of the mechanical age in which we live.

The point is that "things" and "gadgets" are always letting us down. Our car breaks down in the middle of the desert but hums like a hummingbird by the time we get it to the garage. The television conks out with the bases loaded in the bottom of the ninth. The electric can opener quits halfway around a can of spaghetti. The garbage disposal stops working right after rotten apples have been dumped into it.

Even so, we continue to trust things more than people or ideas. All of us probably would be shocked if we were to sit down and calculate the percentage of our incomes we spend on mechanical gadgets which are supposed to make our lives better, easier or more efficient. We do this in spite of the fact that we know most such devices have obsolescence built into them and in the face of many experiences wherein such gadgets have failed to do what they promised. We continue to buy things we don't need with money we don't have to impress people we don't like.

Thus, the *word* for many of us has to be: simplify! simplify! It is not a new word, as is demonstrated by one of the longstanding Quaker Queries: "Do you observe simplicity and moderation in your manner of living?" We know that automatic dishwashers will not save broken marriages, nor will the gift of a dune buggy heal the generation gap. Electric back-massagers will not soothe a troubled spirit, and a Barbie doll that talks will not take the place of a parent who can't talk to his daughter.

To simplify, in short, means to get back to basics—to relationships, to caring, to communication, to sorting out priorities. For what will it profit a man if he gains all the gadgets of the world and still loses his own soul?

O God, Forgive our misplaced priorities that cause us to trust more in gadgets than in You. Help us to be simple-minded and, therefore, wise. In the name of Him who showed us how to live simply. Amen.

ON
TAKING
AIRPLANE
TRIPS

The advancement of modern technology is nowhere more evident than in the field of air transportation. Many young people who have never ridden a train have logged thousands of air miles, and, more significantly, elderly persons by the score routinely fly about the country with few fears and little anxiety.

Good for them. Such a fearless attitude should be encouraged, and far be it from this writer to say anything that might disturb the peace of mind of young or old when it comes to flying in airplanes. Scientific facts support such serenity, and we all know that many more people are killed by slipping in their bathtubs or riding bicycles than die from airplane accidents.

The problem, fellow travelers, is the *concern* for safety that all airlines show which serves to remind us what *can* happen on an airplane if we're not very, very careful. We are told to fasten our seat belts immediately upon arrival, and a pretty stewardess paces up and down the aisle staring discreetly at our abdomens to see that we do. Before the plane even takes off, a small lecture is given on the use of the oxygen mask "in the unlikely event" (as it is stated) such apparatus is needed.

Brief cases and purses cannot be placed overhead, as rough weather may cause them to fall down and break open our heads. Cigarettes are not to be smoked at takeoff or landing, the implication being that gasoline fumes are everywhere and we may all be one puff away from a major explosion. In short, those attractive stewardesses and those dandy demonstrations which are meant to reassure us are counterproductive. Instead of communicating to us that there is nothing to worry about, we may get the message that there is everything to worry about, and lots of people are, in fact, worrying. As we notice the throw-up bag in the seat pocket in front of us and read the "important instructions" provided, wherein we learn that "there are survivors in 60 percent of transport plane accidents," anxieties we didn't know we had may appear faster than we can put up our tray table.

Frequent airplane trips may drive out such fears, of course, but we may also observe how many veteran travelers consume large quantities of alcohol on planes. We may wonder: are they alcoholics, or does the fact that many have two Scotches on the rocks before 10:00 A.M. indicate they know something we do not?

Frequent trips also increase the odds that we will encounter what pilots refer to over their intercoms as "turbulence" and what, to ordinary passengers, becomes an explanation for those paper bags mentioned above.

Flying in an airplane may help us understand the life of faith more clearly. Certainly a rough landing has probably scared more hell out of people than most sermons, but we mean something more profound than this. There is a sense of helplessness about our fate and our lives of which flying in an airplane makes us more aware than most other experiences.

We find ourselves in the hands of nature and its forces, for if the snow is too heavy or the fog too dense, our multi-million dollar plane can't fly. We may be riding in a vehicle which is as powerful as man can produce, but we can still be tossed about by air currents that treat us like chaff blowing in the wind. And we may realize that people we don't know have our very lives in their hands, and if they fail in their responsibilities, there is little we can do about it.

Thus, we may be reminded that life itself—on the ground or in the sky—is a risk. To be alive, in fact, is to be in danger. Only the assurance that God is still running the universe will enable us to experience, in depth, the peace that does not fear even death. Perhaps that sense of peace will make it possible to run risks such as flying in planes—or riding bicycles or taking baths—with ultimate confidence, albeit with nervous moments and sweaty palms right before landing.

O GOD OF THE HEAVENS, Help us to live dangerously without becoming afraid to live. Be very close to pilots, mechanics, stewardesses and all those who make flying airplanes possible. And help us not to be afraid, even when our stomachs are in our mouths. In the name of Him who slept through a storm without fear. Amen.

ON
DEALING
WITH
BUREAUCRACY

To survive in modern America, one must regularly do battle with bureaucracies, both public and private. The great philosophical issue at stake in this struggle is whether business or government will be the first to drive the population to revolution. One can easily understand what Balzac meant when he said that bureaucracy is a giant mechanism operated by Pygmies.

In many counties across the United States, for example, purchasing license plates for one's car has been transformed from a simple exercise into a process so inconsistent and complicated that most people would renounce driving in favor of bicycles were it not so difficult to get a license plate for a bike. One year the would-be driver needs his property tax receipts (which, of course, he's forgotten to bring) in order to purchase his plates. The next year (when he's remembered to bring them), they are not necessary. What is necessary, however, is cash to pay the fee, as personal checks are not accepted (as they were the year before). Bankamericard will be accepted "as a special service to the taxpayers" *if* you carry the credit slips with you, which no living American has ever been known to do. Each change in policy, which is only discovered after an hour's waiting, requires one's forfeiting his place in line to correct the problem, either by returning home to look for the property tax receipts or by rushing to cash a check at a bank which has just closed.

Banks, as a matter of fact, are good examples from the private sector of bureaucracy at work. For years they have been willing to loan large sums of money to people who don't need it, but they at least foreclosed your mortgage or raised your interest rates in a personal way. Some neighborhood institutions were even known to call when checking accounts were overdrawn or when small errors were made on deposit slips. Since many of us often have quite a bit of month left over at the end of the money, this enabled some very personal relationships to be established.

Today computers have taken over such matters. An electronic machine now identifies bad checks the moment your account does not balance. The computer does not know that the check that overdrew your account was the one sent to your wife's father who never thought you'd amount to anything anyway. Nor does it care that you deposited your salary the very day its machine decreed your bankruptcy to the community's grocery and department stores. Complaints about such treatment to a human being, if one is on duty, will be answered by the statement that "the computer now handles our checking operation," an answer that generates a newly felt sympathy for John Dillinger and Clyde Barrow.

The feeling of impotence and rage which the citizen experiences is compounded by the fact that in a bureaucracy the person with whom he deals has no authority to deviate from a policy. The clerk in the license bureau can't cash your check for you, even though there are thousands of dollars in the cash box inches from his hand. The bank teller does not handle overdrawn accounts, and the ex-Marines who do are trained in tactics of intimidation and terror that cause one to lose enthusiasm for protest rather quickly.

What's a citizen to do? More precisely, what's a citizen to do who is committed to practicing Christian principles in his daily affairs and personal relationships? One very long-range hope lies in the fact that bureaucracies, public or private, are eventually purged when enough people decide they've had it and vote the rascals out or take their business elsewhere. The little people will unite when they discover they have nothing to lose but their ulcers.

In the meantime we can seek to live in the world without letting it defeat us. To say, "Thank you very much for calling this to my attention," when the county clerk's office has fined you $2.00 for not having your dog properly tagged, is to live in the grace of God. When, after running four blocks to the license bureau only to see the door closed and locked as you stagger up the steps, you are able to pray: "Thank you, God, for this vigorous exercise," you are well along the path to spiritual maturity, yea, even sainthood!

As difficult as such an attitude is to practice, the alternative is worse. The bureaucracy is the winner when it destroys our sense of humor and causes us to hate its human representatives. We are blessed when we can keep our cool in the face of facelessness, sustained at least slightly by the comforting thought that bankers must buy license plates and bureaucrats keep bank accounts—which serves them right.

O God, We know it will take Your power to straighten out the bureaucracies of our land; it is beyond us. In the interim, give us patience and poise as we deal with people-like computers and computerlike people. In the name of Him whose parents had to go to Bethlehem to pay taxes. Amen.

ON
PROFESSIONAL
MEETINGS

Nearly every business, craft, trade, church, or educational institution has its own professional societies. Many have organizations that have grown up like Topsy, and one cannot help but be impressed by the dedication to vocational excellence these societies represent.

There is everything from the muzzle-loading rifle association, whose members meet regularly to load their muzzles, to taxidermists' organizations, known for their stuffy meetings.[1] Of course, there are medical groups which are as specialized in their meetings as they are in their practice, as obstetricians meet separately from internal medicine men whose constitutions [2] will not allow them to meet together.

1. Sorry about that!
2. Very sorry about that!!

At the present rate of growth in medical societies, one may predict, eye, ear, nose, and throat doctors may require separate gatherings. Hopefully, the nose people will not divide themselves by nostrils, as this would be a truly odorous situation.[3]

It is important to have professional societies, as they enable their members to go to district and national conventions, elect officers, and hear speeches. The best conventions are held in the most inconvenient places, since they are usually a long way from the office. Distance, therefore, gives a rationale for one's absence from his job; and, for example, a secretary will not have to use her vacation time if she is attending the semiannual meeting of left-handed legal secretaries. Furthermore, her boss will not complain, for he knows that he will be attending a convention the next week for officers of corporations which employ left-handed legal secretaries. Indeed, the expensive registration fees, lavish banquets, and extravagant accommodations will be paid for with a smile *and* generous expense accounts, or crossed off as worthy of that secular holy of holies, tax deductibleness.

Workshops are the scheduled events of a convention on which representatives and participants report when they return home. Allegedly, as they say in court, it is in the workshops and seminars that real benefits are derived. Visiting experts usually lead these gatherings, and those in attendance Profit Greatly from the experience. Workshops are usually scheduled in two-hour blocks of time, as this enables conferees to retire to their deductible rooms for naps where they can sleep off the deductible hangover

3. See Romans 7:15-20!!!

from the deductible banquet of the night before. Thus, they, too, Profit Greatly from the experience.

The most highly publicized events at a national meeting are the plenary sessions. Very Important People speak at these, to Call for Action, Appeal for Progress, and Plead for Integrity. Actually, most convention-goers really don't want speeches at all, and many speakers are chosen with this premise in mind. In fact, experienced speakers follow three cardinal rules at conventions: (1) Make it short. (2) Make it funny. (3) Don't interfere with the Happy Hour.

Should one be new to his professional society or lost in the hotel where its convention is being held, he can always tell when he has found the plenary session: practically no one is there. Veteran meeting-goers learn early in the game that one does not go to the Meeting in order to attend the meetings. Only those persons go who were on the planning committee in the first place, or who had very strict toilet training as children and are psychologically unable to deviate from the printed program. Practically everybody else is conspicuous by his absence.

You may wonder where the people are, if they are not hovering near the display booths, participating in the workshops, or attending plenary sessions. Where they are, if not asleep, is in a large but crowded room making business deals or striving to experience Upward Mobility (Job Hunting). The reason men and women go to national conventions is not to learn *what* but to get acquainted with *whom*.

This may be perfectly legitimate, even justifiably tax deductible. But wouldn't it be grand if we didn't have to play games with God, the boss, and the internal revenue service to justify our meetings? Wouldn't it be refreshing to go to a seaside hotel some day and report to the office and to Uncle Sam that we slept late in the morning, played golf all afternoon, and talked only a little business with Charlie Jones over shrimp creole in the evening?

This probably won't happen, but the reason has less to do with our honesty or dishonesty than with our bondage to the belief that play without work cannot really be justified. Many of us, as Wayne Oates says, are "workaholics" who are conditioned to believe that leisure without labor is somehow tainted. Yet, if we work hard much of the time, we ought not to have to justify escape from it and time without it to God or the boss. It may even be that we have moved closer than we know to the Kingdom of God when the day comes that we deliberately skip the business meeting and renew our bodies and souls by going fishing.

O GOD, Help us to know that we can never work hard enough to merit Your gifts to us and that You do not expect us to do so. Help us to accept Your acceptance of us as we are, people who get tired and want to lie in the sun or take a vacation. Enable us to be honest about work and play, especially if we're on an expense account. In the name of Him who was criticized for enjoying himself. Amen.

ON
GOING
TO THE
DENTIST

People waiting in dentists' offices may be the most polite persons in the world. They always seem willing to let the other person go first. Many such hilarious comments have been made about dentistry, as getting a tooth filled or pulled or straightened has long been associated with pain, suffering, and terror.

Such a stereotype, however, is based on an antiquated picture which does not apply today. The vision of a large dentist with a pair of pliers pulling with all his considerable strength to remove what is probably the wrong tooth from the mouth of a helpless and pain-wracked patient is no longer accurate. Today, modern dentists use x-ray machines, high-speed drills, and the most up-to-date methods to remove what is probably the wrong tooth from the mouth of a helpless and pain-wracked patient.

Dentistry is an honorable profession, and most dentists are outstanding citizens who provide many services to the community. Furthermore, the practice of dentistry has eliminated considerable pain from the process in recent years, and stronger pain-killers have helped reduce the suffering as well. Nevertheless, all visitors to the dentist anticipate some suffering, and *the thought* of what lies ahead is similar to the anticipation a heretic had for the inquisition.

High-speed drills, for example, are not machines that bring peace of mind. The instrument sounds like a power saw felling a large tree, and the realization that such noise is produced by activities going on in one's own mouth is a nerve-wracking thought. It may, in fact, wrack some nerves as such drills have been known to strike nerves in molars or bicuspids, causing the patient to scream a lot.

In such circumstances it is difficult to communicate to the dentist that he is causing great pain to your body due to the fact that your mouth is filled with a large wad of absorbent cotton, a clamp to hold the tooth under attack in place, a small air hose to dry out the saliva, and the drill which comes and goes at the discretion of the dentist. Dentists occasionally ask questions of the patient, but they undoubtedly have little interest in the answer, since all answers are the same when you have so much junk in your mouth: "Glub, al-goy fre drib uh. gibble."

Novocaine is given the patient before a tooth is filled or pulled, as we all know. What we tend to forget, however, is that novocaine is not taken in the form of a pill.

It is injected with a needle into the gums, an experience which is much different from a birthday party. It also means that you will have a numb jaw for the next twelve hours, and your friends will wonder why you smile lopsidedly and slobber out of the corner of your mouth.

All of this suffering, both real and imagined, associated with visits to the dentist raises an important question: do the things that are good for us have to hurt? Some people may go to psychiatrists to have their egos stroked, and a few may have surgery for social reasons, but practically nobody goes to have a tooth filled for any other reason than health. Some may even assume that a visit to the dentist would not be worthwhile if there were no pain. It *has* to hurt in order to be good for us.

Such an attitude is not confined to the dentist's office. Many assume the Christian life is like that. If we enjoy ourselves, we feel guilty; for sacrifice, self-denial, and possibly even martyrdom are the "real" forms Christianity should take.

'Tain't necessarily so! One does not live the Christian life in order to be a martyr any more than he visits the dentist to enjoy pain. Both may happen, but the goal of the Christian life is clear: to be a whole person in body, mind, and spirit. There is joy in the Christian life—laughter, fun, jokes, and fellowship. One can be just as "Christian" in these moments as when he is suffering for a worthy cause. He might even experience one of the great moments of happiness that comes too infrequently, that moment of ecstasy when your child says: "Look, dad, no cavities!" Then he will know it doesn't *have* to hurt to be a part of the good life.

O God, Help us to have life and have it more abundantly, even though this will include visits to the dentist. Remind us to live disciplined lives, to brush after meals, and avoid hard candy, that our opportunities for joy may increase. In the name of Him who brought good news. Amen.

ON
LIVING
IN AN
OLD HOUSE

The joys of home ownership are many, and a large number of Americans do not really feel they have a home until they and their friendly neighborhood lending institutions share a mortgage. A rented house or a high-rise apartment is seldom a satisfactory substitute for a vine-covered cottage which symbolizes that a family has roots.

Any homeowner who has lived in the same place for three or more years understands the depth of these feelings and the reason for them. He knows that sentiment is almost always associated with suffering and pain, and homeowners experience considerable quantities of both. They know that vines cause cottages to depreciate badly, and those roots they are putting down will probably clog the drain. Indeed, keeping one's house from collapsing around himself is modern man's bondage, and old houses are particularly harsh masters.

The one in which this writer lives illustrates the point perfectly. Just as Charlie Brown is convinced that there are trees which eat kites, so are we convinced that ours is a people-eating house. Such buildings people-break humans the way humans housebreak dogs. For example, plumbing in old houses usually leaves a little to be desired. We would be better off, in fact, if it left a lot to be desired, because then we could justify hiring a plumber to come and do a major overhaul. As it is, we suffer the tyranny of trivial but perpetual plumbing problems.

Thus, the handle that opens and closes the drain on our tub-shower only works if you hold it down manually. As a consequence, during each shower one finds himself balancing on his left foot while with the other he attempts to keep the drain handle at the open position so that the tub will not overflow. This is not easily done, and grabbing hold of the shower curtain to maintain one's balance has led to some interesting results—that is, if the sight of a naked, middle-aged man pulling a plastic shower curtain down on top of himself as he slips on the soap can be adequately described as "interesting."

The faucets in the sink once dripped for six months and totally resisted all amateur efforts to fix them. During that time the water bill assumed proportions comparable to the national debt and nearly equalled the cost of getting a plumber to come and spend fifteen minutes fixing the damage and repairing our repairs. The downstairs commode gurgles and bubbles after each flushing, and the entire family has had to learn the delicate art of flipping its handle in just the right way to calm its troubled waters. The hot water tank leaks slightly, which keeps the basement perpetually damp, and every time someone turns on the outside faucet to water the grass, air gets into the pipes and for two or three days we are treated to sounds not unlike those of the mating call of an oversexed moose.

Roofs in old houses often leak, but always—it seems—in a sneaky fashion. Usually, the leak is a little one at the peak of the roof from which water runs down and soaks through a plastered wall right over your bed. As a result, the homeowner is continually patching the wrong place. His patching, furthermore, is often less than effective even when he finds the right place, as wrapping a plastic disposal bag around an old piece of linoleum and holding it in place with a cement block is not the procedure accepted by the roofers of America.

If plumbing and roofing miseries do not sufficiently consume all the spare time, energy, and cash of the homeowner, old houses will provide other problems. Overloaded electrical circuits in houses wired shortly after Thomas Edison invented the light bulb cause the owners, as the Bible says, to "see through a glass darkly." Replacing putty in ancient windows is worth at least two Saturday afternoon football games a year, and is second only to painting the kitchen—a task which has undoubtedly increased the number of apartment dwellers in America by 40 percent.

Why do so many choose of their own free will to live in old houses? In addition to some dubious financial considerations, there are also—if we look hard enough—some theological reasons. We don't mean the obvious fact that man learns from adversity, and all that. More to the point, if there is one, is the way in which old houses remind us that the nuisances of life are always with us. A fitting metaphor might be: life is a plastered wall and every day you find another crack.

Just as the owner of an old house will never finally "get it in shape," neither will life be settled so that we will be free of worrisome and irritating problems. Our best hope for happiness is to keep flipping the handles and plugging the holes, while rejoicing in the knowledge that the commode still works, albeit strangely, and the room hasn't leaked since the last time it rained.

O God, Help us to be content with what we have and save our discontent for the problems that matter in Your eyes. May the groaning of the water pipes be music to our ears and a reminder to keep our lives in good repair. In the name of the Carpenter's Son. Amen.

ON
BUYING
LIFE
INSURANCE

When, in the course of human events, a man decides to buy life insurance, he may not really know that which he is doing. He will soon learn, however, that in this cold, impersonal world, someone cares—his life insurance agent. Moreover, he cares for you for what you are—a payer of premiums—and during the time that he is seeking to persuade you to assume the lifelong obligation of an insurance premium, he is second only to the Internal Revenue Service in his concern for you.

One point is clear: insurance agents sincerely do want us to live long, healthy lives. In fact, they take meticulous pains to make sure that we who purchase their policies are not health risks. It is somewhat embarrassing to have complete strangers ask personal questions about our kidneys, liver, and duodenum. Furthermore, it is disconcerting when they, upon inquiring if there is a history of mental illness in one's family, hesitate before accepting an answer of "none." Should we answer the question "When were you last treated by a physician?" with information indicating that we had a bad cold two years previously, we probably will be "accepted" for insurance only as a calculated risk. Even then, should we cough in the agent's presence, rates will probably double automatically.

Life insurance policies should be more comforting than they are, as many of them seem to anticipate strange kinds of eventualities and yet to ignore some of the more likely dangers to your life such as suicide or murder which are commonplace in the experience of married people. Yet, a policy may protect the insured from being trampled by wild buffalo in Borneo or eaten by cannibals after being shipwrecked on one of the South Sea Islands.

The company probably will not be responsible, however, if "the insured" (that's the way you're referred to in insurance policies) gets less than twelve hours of sleep per night or participates in any strenuous exercise—such as chess or silent prayer. It will be responsible, of course, if you live the "proper" kind of life, and those persons who assume vows of temperance, celibacy, modesty, solvency, and low-cholesterol diets will surely be insured. Once insured, too, agents are able to generate new business for themselves by rewriting your policies. You discover, with their help, that the plan you thought would take care of your family's needs in the event of your death will not do so ten years after purchase because inflation has devalued the dollar. Or, you will be encouraged to change your policy from leaving dividends to accumulate to a program of annuities which guarantee you an income of $37.50 a month for as long as you live. Of course, if you have only $37.50 a month on which to live, you probably won't live very long.

Such is the insured life, but there is an analogy here which will undoubtedly be overlooked if we do not call it to your attention. Many people regard church membership as a kind of spiritual insurance policy. More than one preacher, carried away perhaps by his own rhetoric, has declared that John 3:16 is the best form of life insurance, the implication being that signing on a church's dotted line sometime and someplace will guarantee everlasting benefits from that big claims office in the sky.

Others suggest that church membership, again, like an insurance company, will bring you peace of mind, contentment, and a lifetime of positive thoughts. One well-known writer of newspaper columns has even posed the mind-bending question, "Did you ever know anyone who has died in church?" The inference we are to draw, presumably, is that church attendance wards off death, a somewhat untenable position when all the evidence is considered.

The point is, fellow insured ones, that the Christian life provides no guarantees that we will escape death or find peace of mind or live longer. It is a matter of daily, conscientious, and frequently disturbing decision-making, according to the best light we have within us. Church membership signifies that you are a member of a group which is struggling to live in the Spirit of Christ, not that you have religious group insurance with a special rider regarding fire protection. If we remember this, perhaps we will have lives worth insuring—and worth living.

DEAR GOD, Help us to live lives so much in Your Spirit that when we die even the funeral director will be sorry. Help us not to treat our religion as if it were insurance, so that we will be able to live with risks worth taking in Christ's name. In the name of Him who helped us to see the abundant life being lived. Amen.

ON
SUCCEEDING
IN COLLEGE

One of the most sobering facts to hit educators between the eyes in recent years is the discovery that thousands of persons have graduated from college without knowing anything. Check that. They obviously do know one thing: how to graduate without knowing anything. They have gone beyond Socrates' famous statement, "The wise man is the one who knows that he does not know." They have demonstrated by getting a degree that the wise guy is, indeed, the one who knows he doesn't know but who doesn't let others know it, too.

This is made possible by observance of certain basic rules. First, they always take the initiative. The students who master this skill always *ask* questions during class discussions; they never answer them. While any question is better than an answer, the best ones are of a special kind. These are the questions that give the appearance of there having been extensive reading or research. For example, if the class is examining a certain play or novel, the alert student may ask (with the brow wrinkled in a penetrating look): "But what did Joseph Wood Krutch say about this?" or, "Would you please explain your terms?" In this way the burden of knowledge is always placed on the other guy, who probably hasn't done his reading either; and the rest of the class sits there thinking, "Gee, I wish I knew who Joseph Wooden Crunch was."

Students wise to the ways of *academia* always appear at class a few minutes early and seem deeply engrossed in a book the teacher has placed on the recommended, but not required, reading list. If the professor fails to notice him, he will probably ask him to explain a passage in it. There is usually little difficulty in finding appropriate passages, as the student has undoubtedly read only the chapter headings and the author's preface. Nevertheless, such seeming thirst for the Pierian spring will surely be rewarded.

A second rule of behavior such students follow is called "pamper the professor." A man-to-pedagogue relationship is maintained at all times. Students know that nearly all college teachers regard themselves as humorists who could have been successful entertainers were they not so dedicated to the higher values of life. Thus, whenever a teacher mutters something which he obviously considers clever, the alert student will laugh aloud. Especially alert students will never burst forth with a loud guffaw, of course, because professors consider their humor to be subtle and esoteric, never slapstick. The wisest students grin wryly and shake slightly, perhaps with the head lowered, as if they were sharing a private joke with the teacher. It matters not that others in the room think both these students and the professor are a bunch of simple jerks. The point is that one of the simple jerks gives the grades.

When a student disagrees with the prof, the more insightful ones will cast looks of scorn in his direction. They will also carry their teacher's latest book with them, usually with a worn bookmark sticking out. If he hasn't written any books, the astute student will suggest he write one or, if he can do so with a straight face, he may encourage his professor to publish his lectures. Such helpful suggestions almost always lead to a passing grade, for what college teacher could possibly give poor marks to a student who regards him as a paragon of knowledge and wit? It would be questioning the student's judgment—which obviously is sound.

Finally, the student who survives to get his degree learns that he must study just a little. If he can make himself an expert in one narrow area, he can probably use it to write term papers in several different fields. Knowledge of the Book of Job has been known to carry some students through classes in religion, English, philosophy, and history.

Students who graduate read *about* the assignment in a review or college outline book. They learn enough to be vague, for they know the teacher will probably say for them what he wanted to hear in the first place. Latin footnotes and Greek references add dignity to term papers and are well received in liberal arts schools. Diplomas are usually in Latin, too, and getting them is, after all, the name of the game.

Because the caricature described above is partly true, there is a message for all who claim to be "seekers after truth." It reveals our sham as we remember how we were as students and perhaps recall all those times we "put one over" on the teacher who probably put a few over on his teachers on the way to becoming one himself. Indeed, the educational process itself refutes the claims that knowledge can save us. By itself, it cannot. The will as well as the intellect, the heart as well as the mind, are intricately involved in our desire to be free. Thus, wherever a teacher is instructing students that two apples plus two apples equals four apples, we can be sure that some of those apples are going to be polished before a degree is granted.

OUR FATHER, Forgive us our phoniness, especially when we claim to be seekers after truth. Help us to love You with our minds and our hearts. In the name of Him who was called Teacher by His disciples. Amen.

ON
ALUMNI
APPEALS

One of the fringe benefits of attending educational institutions is the inevitability of receiving letters for the rest of your life asking for donations. Since most Americans attend high school, trade schools, undergraduate colleges, graduate institutions, and occasionally take a two-week seminar someplace else (which puts them on still another mailing list), the opportunity to support education with our dollars is never far from us.

Indeed, when we multiply the above involvements by our spouses' educational connections, add the latest appeal from a local community college starting in the towns where we live, and find ourselves confronted by the needs of the schools our children have chosen to attend, we may very well feel like the Ford Foundation—Edsel division!

What's an alumnus or alumna, as the case may be, to do?

(1) He can cry a lot, a response which is not necessarily inappropriate, although helpful only to the one who cries. There is some reason to shed tears, especially if one is a graduate of a private institution. Colleges and universities are living from hand to mouth, and any financial discussion by college officials sounds much like a command performance of *The Beggar's Opera*. A good appeal letter these days is measured by the number of Kleenex tissues used after reading it.

(2) Another alternative is to give a small amount. Many alumni have done so for several years, and this proves to be an effective response. Giving a small amount gets other would-be recipients off one's back and enables the donor to be honest when he refuses their appeals on the grounds that he already gave to his old Alma Mater. This also enables him to maintain his sincerity, which is absolutely essential, for once he has learned to fake sincerity, he will be able to have an impressive public image without its costing him a large sum of money.

(3) Of course, we can make a gift to our favorite educational institution a high priority matter. We can give sacrificially and That Sort of Thing. We can "share vicariously," as the appeal letter puts it, in the efforts of the school to shape the future of America by contributing to the swimming pool fund or the Snodgrass Memorial Chair of Applied Psychology. If we really get carried away, we help "set men free" (liberal arts language), provide leaders in the race for technological supremacy (engineering schools), or get our names on a bronze plaque near the entrance to the fieldhouse (all NCAA schools).

(4) We can become class agents and write an appeal letter ourselves. Alumni officials favor such a response because the writer almost always becomes a giver. The moment he sets his pen to the paper to ask a classmate for a dollar, he will begin to feel subtle (but real) moral pressure from the entire alumni association, the school faculty, the Board of Trustees, and the Church Universal to Give More. In short, if one has problems of resisting alumni appeals that come through the mail, he must never (repeat: *never*) consent to write such a letter himself. It will cost him his previously modest giving record and thwart his best efforts to maintain warm feelings for the old school at a low cost.

Actually, there is no easy solution, as the problems of survival for colleges are genuine and many schools are dying every year. The only choices we have are to give more, or give something, or give lots. We'll still have to live with our guilt feelings, of course, or come up with some creative rationalizations for not giving this year. Nevertheless, it could be worse. We could have gone to Harvard, instead of Yale (or vice versa). And how would you have liked to be asked to support *them?*

O LORD, We thank You that we are able to be touched by appeals for help from places that are worthy and seek, in some degree, to do Your will. Help us not to be soft touches, however, so that the colleges won't waste money on foolish and unnecessary junk. Help us to seek first Your Kingdom and not bronze plaques. In the name of Him who compared Pharisees and publicans with surprising results. Amen.

ON
GIVING
TILL
IT HURTS

In this precarious and uncertain world, few things are sure. Traditionally, only death and taxes have been considered unavoidable. All other matters are likely to change "in the twinkling of an eye," as the Bible says. However, one more item needs to be added to that rather short list of "unchanging facts of life." It is the cold realization that sooner or later, someplace or somehow, we will all be asked to buy something we don't need with money we don't want to spend to help somebody we don't know.

It may be Girl Scout cookies (the peanut butter ones are excellent!) or Boy Scout candy. Perhaps the knock on the door will be a club member selling tickets to a lacrosse game or chances on a car. We mustn't overlook the Community Fund, the Red Cross, UNICEF, or that kid across the street who, if he sells enough magazine subscriptions, will win a six-day trip to Detroit to smell the smog.

Churches, it seems, are strongly tempted to get involved in this capitalistic enterprise almost before they realize it. Like natives on a South Pacific island who earn their livings by taking in each other's laundry, church members support their worthy causes by selling things to each other. We have almost returned to a bartering system, and we may soon find ourselves in a situation in which no money changes hands at all, just commodities. Handmade aprons could be traded for salt-water taffy with a rate of exchange established and figured in terms of green stamps.

Who knows where it will end? If money-raising projects continue to dominate the work of churches, perhaps we should equip ourselves properly for our tasks. Instead of membership being based on statements of faith, we could ask newcomers to endorse our products. Instead of assigning them to the usual committees, we could sign them up for management training, promotional techniques or sales conferences. The really big influential churches might even be listed on the stock market.

All this, however, is written with tongue-in-cheek, as we all know churches today are no worse than those fellows who sold pigeons to sacrifice in the temple in Jesus' day. And even there the analogy stops, excepting the fact that both were tax-exempt. As the Quakers say, what's a little bargaining among Friends?

The point is, fellow hucksters, that we do need to examine the motives and attitudes behind these efforts. We have to ask: Do our ends really justify our means? Do our means justify themselves? Do we neglect other matters more important because of our preoccupation with projects and profits?

Am I selling fruit cakes because the income goes to a worthy cause, or is it because I got caught by the project chairman before I could sneak out the side door? Do these efforts cause friction, dissension, and discontent, and do they take the place of visiting the sick, helping the poor in personal ways, or practicing genuine stewardship?

The sociologists tell us that one of the main handicaps under which local churches and individual members labor is the confusion of "survival goals" with "formal goals." In other words, we confuse money-raising projects with the real work of the church, namely, increasing the love of God and the love of neighbor. The work of the church and church work are, unfortunately, not always the same. Money, donated or raised by projects, is always needed for the causes the church embraces, but equally important— nay, more important—is the involvement of people in the problems of the world in personal ways. We need to visit the sick and the prisoners, comfort the bereaved, listen to the distressed, and speak to the lonely. Projects, however, can't substitute for such a ministry.

Those who bear the name "Christian" can never regard the neighbor whom Christ tells us to love as a potential customer or part of a consumer market out there somewhere. Yes, we need money to carry on the work of the Kingdom of God, but we can never forget it is the Kingdom of God for which we are working, not a tidy profit on the week's receipts.

ETERNAL GOD, Help us to be more than hucksters, hustling pennies in Your name. So fill us with the vision of what Your church is and ought to be that we will be the Body of Christ and not merely busybodies. In the name of Him who cleansed the temple. Amen.

ON
GIVING
GIFTS
AT CHRISTMAS

If the Wise Men had known what they were starting, they might not have brought gifts in the first place. Gift giving at Christmas, however, has gotten so far out of hand that it has become a major factor in retail selling. Traditionally ministers are supposed to oppose such commercialism, even though few people, including ministers themselves, pay much attention. Thus, if we can't beat them, perhaps we should join them. Here, therefore, are several gift suggestions, fellow shoppers, all taken from advertisements in reputable magazines and newspapers.

You might want to consider giving someone you love an imported camel saddle, a giant 12-foot meteorological balloon, or even a mink lid cover for the well-dressed powder room. For the businessman on your list, or your boss, you could choose an "executive pencil box" which has special compartments for such necessities as pills, paper clips, washroom key, and a "tension reducer." It does not, however, have a place for erasers, for "executives do not make mistakes."

If $200 gold watchbands are beyond your budget, you may want to show the One in your life you really care by presenting him with a solid gold toothpick ($14.30). If the One has no teeth but likes the prestige of owning gold, you may want to present him or her with solid gold garters.

Friends or enemies who have pets would be thrilled to add to their menageries with either a pet monkey or live sea horses at $1.00 each. You can also buy genuine diapers for parakeets, a really different gift which special friends will remember for years—especially if they don't have any parakeets.

For those relatives who seem to have everything, we humbly suggest the truly unique gift, one which epitomizes Christmas giving in the Twentieth Century and the spirit behind it as well as any gift we know. Called "The Eternal Revenue Man," it is best described by the very words of the advertisement which called it to our attention. "The Eternal Revenue Man is a little box with a tiny holder on it where your friends can place a coin of any denomination. Immediately, you hear a grinding of gears . . . the box starts shaking . . . slowly the lid rises and a pale green hand reaches out, grabs the coin, quickly pulls it inside and 'Bang!' the lid slams shut. That's all it does . . . takes the money and hides it away." The ad for this gift concluded, appropriately, with this comment: "You'll be amazed how much your friends will contribute and it's non-reportable income!"

The amazing fact is to learn that there really are buyers of such gifts and people who enjoy receiving them! It is, of course, difficult to see a connection between these absurdities and gifts given by the Wise Men to the Child of Bethlehem. Yet, the extreme nature of such gifts may have a redemptive message for us. Perhaps such unusual and absurd gifts symbolize the difficulty we all share when we seek to express affection, love, loyalty or appreciation.

What we want to say by our gifts is usually something so personal that, even if it is only a white handkerchief, we hope it will be remembered as if it were special. There is a need within us to communicate to those whom we love that our feelings for them are special and real. Furthermore, there is a need within us to make peace with those whom, most of the year, we've treated casually or thoughtlessly. The fact that the commercialism of our society exploits such needs should not overshadow the reality of their existence.

Solid gold toothpicks probably will not express such feelings any better than, or as well as, a commonplace gift we give with a gracious spirit. The important thing, however, is that we never stop trying to express how we feel toward the other human beings who share our lives. For as one person learns how to tell—or show—others that he really cares, he will also have learned much of what the coming of Christ really means.

O GOD OF CHRISTMAS, Forgive us for treating people casually, both by thoughtless deeds and in deedless thoughts. Help us at Christmas to find the ways of expressing our love which will say what we mean. Help us, too, to discover Your love so that we can mean what we say. In the name of the One who gave Himself. Amen.

ON
ELECTION YEAR
TENSIONS

By and large, Christians get along well with one another. They gather in their churches on Sunday with a minimum of disagreement, and most serious conflicts are set aside for denominational meetings on unity.

The exception to this is during election years. Some church members will forgive their fellows of theft, murder, and embezzlement, but they may never be able to understand how a person can be a Christian *and* a Democrat (or vice versa) at the same time. Upon learning that some among the baptized brethren are actually of the opposite political faith, they can only shake their heads in dismay and assume that either brain damage or high blood pressure confuses their minds at election time.

Hard-core, genuine, honest-to-goodness, passionate Republicans and Democrats are convinced that the issues between them are much broader than simply the way one casts his ballot in the privacy of the voting booth. It has to do with the very stuff of life, and—they think—one ought to be able to identify Republicans and Democrats by the way they live their lives.

Democrats tend to think of themselves as the more open-handed party. Republicans agree. You have to have an open hand, they say, in order to reach into somebody else's pockets. They, in turn, think of themselves as more frugal and tight-fisted. Again, surprisingly, there is agreement from the Democrats. The Republicans already have theirs, they point out, and they're not going to let anyone take it away. Thus, Democrats make plans, then do something else. Republicans follow plans their grandfathers made. Republicans study financial pages of the newspaper, while Democrats use them to line the bottom of bird cages. Democrats name their children after currently popular sports figures, politicians, and entertainers. Republican children are named after their parents and grandparents, according to where the most money is.

Republicans are regarded by their Democratic critics as being solemn, stuffy, and pompous. In response, members of the Grand Old Party look upon the Democrats as frivolous and irresponsible. Convinced that Democrats buy most of the books that have been banned somewhere, Republicans form censorship committees and read them as a group. Democrats assume that Republicans post all the signs saying No Trespassing and Cars Will Be Towed away at Violator's Expense; therefore, they bring their picnic baskets and start bonfires with the signs.

Republicans tend to keep their shades drawn, although

there is seldom any reason why they should. Democrats, say GOP members, ought to but don't. Republican boys date Democratic girls, even though they plan to marry Republican girls. However, they feel they're entitled to a little fun first. Once married, Republicans sleep in twin beds—some even in separate rooms. That's why there are so many more Democrats.

Confirmed Republicans and Democrats claim to be able to identify the other by their leisure-time activities. Republicans fish from the stem of a chartered boat while Democrats sit on the dock and let the fish come to them. When they're done fishing, Democrats clean and eat what they've caught. Republicans hang them on the wall. On Saturdays, Republicans head for the country club and the Democrats go bowling. At home, the Democrats watch crime and Western shows on television, which make them clench their fists and become red in the face; Republicans get the same effect from Presidential press conferences, especially if a Democrat is in office. If a Republican is in office, there probably won't be any press conferences.

All persons who go to church early in the morning are Democrats, but those you see coming out of white wooden churches are surely Republicans. Most Democrats and Republicans do not go to church at all, but their reasons for not going are different. The Republicans are up early to play golf, while the Democrats are still in bed recovering from an all-night pinochle game. The Democrats in a church will give their worn-out clothes to those less fortunate than they. The Republicans will wear theirs a little longer.

Such stereotypes as the above, of course, are only

partially true, but they may serve at least one good purpose. They may help remind us that ultimate loyalties must be reserved for Ultimate Beings, and when we think the saved and the damned are identifiable by political affiliation, we have made a significant mistake. In fact, Jesus may have spoken of the *Kingdom* of God rather than the *Republic* of God in order to help Christians avoid fighting with one another at election time.

ETERNAL GOD, Keep us from confusing our political beliefs with Your Truth. Enable us to work in politics with a spirit of love and tolerance, and enlighten my brother, Frank, in his political views before election day—if it be Your will. In the name of Him who got crucified by the party in power. Amen.

ON
DEMONIC
POWERS

Once upon a time I visited my brother in New York City. While admiring his newly decorated and beautifully furnished apartment, I managed (1) to stand up suddenly and break the ceramic globe on an $80.00 lamp; (2) spill grape juice on his new walnut table; and (3) drop melted butter on his recently carpeted and (formerly) blue floor. In that moment I came to understand what that great contemporary prophet, F. Wilson, meant when he said, "The devil made me do it!"

Other similar occasions rush quickly to mind, moments when I felt sure demons were after me. There was the time I had a flat tire while rushing to an appointment, the repairing of which took place only after the car had fallen off the jack twice and which caused me to phone ahead in order to explain my tardiness. In this attempt I discovered I had no change for the pay phone and had to get the proper coins from a nearby tavern, the proprietor of which seemed to think I had come to rob her, which delayed my call, which was never completed because the phone was out of order. My frustration level in decibels on that occasion was matched only by the time I inadvertently dragged the sleeve of my suit coat through the commode of a rest room of a hotel where I was scheduled, fifteen minutes later, to give a speech.

If demonic powers are picking on us, perhaps we should put them to work. Should farmers need rain for their crops, we could plan a picnic or some similar activity, the enjoyment of which requires dry and sunny weather. Great torrents of rain will undoubtedly come, and the only danger will be flooding.

If you, faithful reader, experience frustration from time to time in trying to find a place to park your car in downtown shopping districts, simply call some of us whom the devils are pursuing. We will travel in the opposite direction from you, but toward the destination you have in mind, because all empty parking places are always located on the opposite side of the street, adjacent to a No U-Turn sign.

If you would like to meet some distinguished people, drop by our house on a day when the refrigerator is being defrosted, the furniture is being rearranged, the children are finger-painting, and the aquarium has just sprung a leak. You can be sure on such a day that a college president, a prospective benefactor of the Earlham School of Religion, or my wife's old boyfriend will appear to make a social call.

We'll be glad to introduce you to such dignitaries, and you can talk to them while we change from our ragged and paint-smeared shorts and attempt to wipe the mowing machine oil from our hands, some of which will undoubtedly have been transferred to the hands of the visitors.

The above scene, of course, is not a true picture of events. Life is really much worse! Like Job, we may wonder why we get picked on so much. We may assume that our own frustrations and pain are sufficient proofs that the demonic forces of the world are in control.

Thus, we need to relearn what Job also learned. Contrary to the feeling of picked-upon-ness that we have, the world does not rotate around *us*. *We* are not the center of the universe but merely part of the stream of life which, while polluted, is still drinkable. The person who thinks *his* life is the hardest, *his* problems the greatest, or *his* frustrations unique may have begun to think the world revolves about him. Christian humility comes when we realize that faithfulness to God does not set us free from problems and frustrations; it enables us to grow by the way in which we *respond* to them. Such a message, in fact, is what this little book has been about. If we are able to see life this way, we will probably not rid ourselves of demons, but we may be able to tame them. And a demon which becomes a household pet need not be feared.

O God, Help us not to take our pet problems and frustrations too seriously. Enable us to take what comes and learn from it, whether it be a flat tire or a broken heart. In the name of Him who drove out demons. Amen.